Ken Bernstein

JPMGUIDES

Contents

Hand of Fatima, a good-luck sign

This Way Tunisia

Awakening

Very early on the morning of your first full day in Tunisia, it begins to sink in that this is an altogether exotic place. You might well be awakened before dawn by the chant of the muezzin loudspeakered from a nearby minaret. Is it a dream? You sink back to sleep, lulled by the sound of the lapping sea and the twittering birds. The next awakening is the chatter of the hotel staff; it sounds like an argument, but that's just the unfamiliar sounds of Arabic. Breakfast, though, is as comforting as authentic *café au lait* and fresh, fragrant *croissants*.

The bewildering contrasts of the familiar and the foreign add spice to the Tunisian experience. The people are dignified and friendly, with a quick sense of humour. But most women hide all but their faces from public view. (In homes and offices, though, they are more liberated than you think.)

Preconceptions are bowled over by the Tunisian superlatives. You assume you'll be dragged to see humdrum historic sites, but you are stirred by the ancient wonders of Carthaginian and Roman civilizations (many of them listed by UNESCO as World Heritage Sites). You have been promised good beaches, but you can hardly believe the infinity of powdery sand. You may have expected a rigid veiled society, but you find the most tolerant, welcoming people.

From the Mediterranean shores to the Sahara, Tunisia is one big sunny surprise.

Geography Lesson

It's the smallest and most relaxed North African nation, at a longitude halfway between the Strait of Gibraltar and the island of Crete. With an area of 163,610 sq km (63,170 sq miles) Tunisia is a bit smaller than Washington State or Missouri, and about twice the size of Austria or Ireland. The country has only two neighbours, Algeria to the west and Libya to the southeast. The northern and eastern extremities face the Mediterranean Sea.

With its feet in the Sahara and its head in the Med, Tunisia covers a lot of scenic ground. In the north the velvety hillsides might remind you of Europe at its most bountiful. The south lives up to everybody's image of a desert of dunes interrupted by green oases, where the dates come from. As for beaches, Tunisia's 1,300-km

(800-mile) share of the Mediterranean shore runs from hidden coves to endless white sand beaches that nature's generous master plan might have designed for children.

Towns and Villages

Tunis, the national capital, claims a metropolitan population of 1.6 million inhabitants—about one in six of the nation's total. It suffers some of the inconveniences of a big city, especially traffic jams (four times a day). It also has a very civilized tree-shaded promenade down the middle of the main street, a lively, labyrinthine medieval medina, and one of the world's outstanding museums.

In Sfax, the country's second-most populous city, the modern heart of town is something of a charmer, in spacious French colonial style, and the walled medina is thoroughly lived-in.

The holy city of Kairouan turns out to have much more to offer than a mosque of humbling grandeur. The everyday life of the city, the animated medina, and superlative folkloric shopping explain the relentless press of the tourist throngs.

And so on down to the merest village, with its modest mosque and minaret and a main street shared by a few cars, a smoky bus, seemingly aimless pedestrians, and perhaps sheep, goats and camels, as well. "Café society" here starts at sunrise when the local chaps gather at the café—not for a fast coffee on the way to the office, but just to gather. It goes on all day; the womenfolk stay at home.

Beyond the Beach

That lovely coastline inevitably prompts thoughts of swimming and sunbathing. To make the most of the sea, all manner of water sports are on tap: sailing, windsurfing, fishing or scuba diving; you can even take a ride in a submarine. Many luxury hotels

---

1

THE BEST MUSEUM There are several first-class museums around the country, especially at Carthage and Sousse, but nothing can match the **Bardo Museum** in Tunis. It's so rich in Roman relics that some sarcophagi that other museums would put on prominent display are used as flower boxes. From prehistoric relics to popular arts of the Islamic era, all the glory of Tunisia is on show—in the Bey's palace, no less.

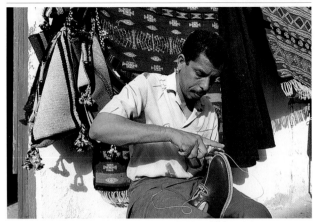

All done by hand: a shoemaker at work in Douz, the gate to the Sahara.

now specialize in thalasso-therapy, installing state-of-the-art spa facilities to tone up those flabby muscles.

On dry land, the resorts have dozens of tennis courts. Golf is becoming a big deal from Tabarka to Monastir, with several new courses under construction. Horseback riding is very special when it's along a gently sloping beach or through desert-style underbrush.

Or you can get to know a camel, for an hour or a matter of days trekking from oasis to oasis.

Part of the Tunisian adventure is the shopping: haggling over a rug in a souk is surely a long way from the usual souvenir hunt. And if you find, eventually, that your budgie hates the palatial bird-cage you bought, you still have the memory of the salesman who poured a round of mint tea and convinced you it would be the best buy of your life.

What about nightlife? They have organized everything from desert folklore festivals to belly-dancers. If the local music strikes you as an interminable drone of minor-key meanderings, you'll find more familiar fare blaring at the hotel disco. And it goes on as late as you like.

It's just too bad about that wake-up call.

5

Restitution of an internal view of the ANTONIAN
Baths at the end of the 2nd C.A.D.

Flashback

Scenes from History

Up and down the land that is now Tunisia, Stone Age wanderers left their footprints, tools and weapons. Here the clock of prehistory goes back nearly as far as an archaeologist's imagination, say hundreds of thousands of years.

Written history doesn't start until a mere 3,000 years ago, when Phoenicians from what is now Lebanon arrived in a land long occupied by Berber tribes. They founded a trading base at Utica, and then the mighty city of Carthage (meaning, prosaically, "New Town"). The wily Carthaginians tangled once too often with the Caesars of Rome, and then Carthage was annihilated. For centuries thereafter a pattern of siege, violence and conquest bloodied the land. There was no lack of drama at the hands of Romans, Vandals, Barbary pirates, Normans, Turks, and, during more recent times, the French. It's a long story, as complex and inextricable as a map of the medina.

It's not so difficult to picture the glory that once was Carthage.

Carthage

In the 9th century BC the Carthaginians established their capital along the sea within commuting distance of what would become Tunis. From this vast walled city Carthage ruled not a conventional empire but a lucrative web of Mediterranean commerce, and the good times lasted for seven centuries. For all its derring-do, Carthage's reputation was tarnished by the society's obsessive business goals, lack of artistic innovation, and devotion to a religion that involved human sacrifices.

As Carthage expanded into the growing Roman sphere of influence, three famous wars ensued. General Hannibal was the superhero when he and his elephants crossed the Alps into Rome's home base in the second Punic war, but the third round ended in disaster in 146 BC. Celebrating their victory over Carthage, the unforgiving Romans destroyed the city, salted the earth, and made slaves of the survivors.

Roman Days

Thank Julius Caesar for the reconstruction of Carthage from ground zero. Just over a century after the city was wiped out, the emperor surveyed the site and decided it was too good to waste on revenge. The new Carthage became the administrative headquarters of the Roman province of Africa. With a population that reached 300,000 it rated as the third-biggest city in the empire (after Rome and Alexandria). All over Tunisia—as splendid ruins now reveal—the Romans thought big and founded many grand outposts. Under Roman rule Christianity came to Tunisia, first as a clandestine cult, later as an important, legal religion. The sins that St Augustine catalogued in his *Confessions* were committed in wicked Carthage.

The Dark Ages engulfed Tunisia in the 5th century AD when the Vandals roared in from Europe. As inept as they were cruel, the Germanic hordes set the stage for anarchy. To fill the vacuum the Byzantine emperor Justinian sent an invasion force that drove out the barbarians. Byzantine rule lasted 150 years, long enough to leave archaeologists some fine churches and forts.

Arabian Nights

Within a century of the death of the Prophet Mohammed in AD 632, fervent Arab Muslim armies had conquered North Africa, the Middle East, Spain and even part of France. In Tunisia a series of Arab invasions proved inconclusive until the very end of the 7th century when Oqba ibn Nafi finally put down Berber resistance, defeating (and beheading) a dynamic queen, the Jewish prophetess Kahina. The conqueror went on to create Kairouan as his desert capital. It became one of the holy sites of Islam.

The Aghlabid dynasty ruled Tunisia for all of the 9th century, building forts and sumptuous mosques at home and invading pagan territories abroad. Sicily still credits the Aghlabids with planting melons and citrus fruits and building a sophisticated irrigation system.

Medieval Upheaval

Dynasty followed dynasty in medieval Tunisia. Even the far-flung 12th-century Normans, under Roger II, otherwise King of Sicily, came in and ruled for a decade, tolerantly. The Almohads from Morocco, who drove out the Normans, brought some culture and prosperity to the countryside. Then the Hafsids held power for more than three centuries, keeping Tunisia independent. Hafsid rulers didn't hesitate to call themselves Caliphs, thus claiming to be successors to the Prophet. The pious king of France, Louis IX, leading a crusade against the Tunisian Muslims, came down with the plague

Ancient Roman grandeur touched Tunisia as far afield as El Djem.

in Carthage and died. The Crusades were called off for good, and the lamented Louis was propelled to sainthood.

After 1492

More than seven centuries of struggle between Muslims and Christians in Spain ended in 1492 when Ferdinand and Isabella finally expelled the Moors from their last redoubt, Granada. Keeping up the pressure, their grandson, the Habsburg Emperor Charles V, lashed out at North African ports. Tunisia enlisted corsairs like the celebrated Barbarossa to repel the attackers, then invited the Ottoman Empire

to help. The Turks threw out the Spaniards but installed their own appointees as rulers of Tunisia. The system lasted for more than a century, and then in 1704 an Ottoman Turk, Hussein ibn Ali Turki, pronounced himself hereditary ruler. The beys that followed, all his descendants, continued to reign, if loosely, until as recently as the 1950s.

During the Ottoman era, Tunisia's seafaring tradition—the unkind word would be piracy—brought the country fame and wealth. The corsairs employed powerful oarsmen to manoeuvre their galleys all but invisibly to the kill, snatching prisoners and 9 booty from ill-defended ships or vulnerable ports. But it's the Berbers, not barbarians, who account for the Barbary Coast's name.

Hard Times

In the early 19th century European powers teamed up to eliminate the pirates, which was bad for the Tunisian balance of payments. So were the extravagances of Bey Ahmed I, such as the oversized army he conscripted; on the humanitarian side, he did outlaw slavery.

As the economy declined, Tunisian sovereignty was whittled away. In 1857 Europeans were permitted to own land. Financial affairs grew so grave that England, France and Italy took over the fiscal strings of the bankrupt state. Whopping new taxes inspired unrest. The British bowed to French ambitions in Tunisia, whereupon France elbowed Italy aside, sending in an expeditionary force and proclaiming a French Protectorate in 1881. The French brought order to Tunisia, and built roads.

Towards Independence

Almost from the moment the French seized control, Tunisians began mobilizing to regain control of their destiny. The "Young Tunisian Party", formed in 1907, met a stone wall. After World War I, Destour, the elitist Constitutional Party, tried to negotiate with the French but in vain. In 1934 militants formed the Neo-Destour party, headed by a radical Sorbonne-educated lawyer, Habib Bourguiba. This won him the first of his prison sentences.

In World War II Tunisia was the scene of an armoured battlefield drama; the Allies won. The Free French forces regained control, rejecting the renewed agitation for a Free Tunisia. After widespread violence and years of negotiations, Tunisia attained internal self-rule in 1955 and then independence.

The Republic

The first independent government was formed by Bourguiba. In 1957 the Bey was deposed and Tunisia became a republic. As the George Washington of modern Tunisia, Bourguiba was repeatedly elected president, and finally President for Life. In 1987 he was pronounced senile and removed from office and succeeded by his Prime Minister, Zine el-Abidine Ben Ali. Tunisia in the past decade was sensitive to the tensions electrifying the area, aiming for stability, justice and progress in an unpredictable world.

Beyond the stony gaze, recollections of Carthage's past.

On the Scene

Geographers slice Tunisia in various ways, most simplistically in three: the fertile north; the central coast and its bucolic plain; and the south, which soon melts into the Sahara. It's much more complicated, but this guide covers the country in five chapters, starting with the populous Bay of Tunis area and ending in the wide open spaces of the deep south. Try to see as much as you can. The variety of physical features, from craggy mountains to salt lakes, is staggering. And history is everywhere.

▶ BAY OF TUNIS
Tunis, Carthage, Sidi Bou Saïd

The metropolitan area of Tunis covers so much ground, and so many centuries, that you may need a cure for culture shock. Tunis itself, the capital and biggest city of the country, is in the present tense—high-rises, modern tramway and all—but superimposed on layers of the distant past. And the suburbs range from the wonders of ancient Carthage (interspersed with many flower-decked modern villas) to the most photographed white village in Tunisia, Sidi Bou Saïd, so charming it's almost mythical.

The minaret of Zitouna, the Great Mosque, is a 19th-century addition.

Your first impression of Tunis is likely to be the efficient, late-20th-century airport, or the sea-port, which started as a medieval feat of engineering. To get your bearings, though, stroll beneath the subtropical canopy of starling-infested fig trees lining the main boulevard of the modern city. Until an ambitious reclamation project of the late 19th century it was all under water, part of the marshy Lake of Tunis.

Tunis
Under the French protectorate the modern district of Tunis took rather stately form—a promenade striding proudly from the gate of the medina to the edge of

the port, a grand compound for the colonial powers, and a grid of shopping streets reminiscent of a provincial city someplace in southern France.

The main boulevard starts as Avenue de France, where the palatial French embassy faces the twin-towered Roman Catholic cathedral. Built in the 1880s, the Cathedral of St Vincent de Paul is a cocktail of architectural styles climaxed by a God-like sculpture with outstretched hands, unusual anywhere but startling in a culture that outlaws graven images.

Avenue Habib Bourguiba

Sooner or later, everyone is bound to turn up along this mercifully shaded promenade, taking the air, buying flowers or an ice cream, a book or a newspaper, or sitting on a bench to watch the world go by. And what a world! There are women wrapped up in white *haiks*, hiding everything but half a face, and women decked out in Paris fashions, men in burnooses or in fitted sports jackets and school ties.

On both sides of the avenue are modern stores, hotels, travel agencies and cafés; a phalanx of shoeshine men work the arcades on the south side. At the eastern extremity of the boulevard there used to be an equestrian statue of then-President Bourguiba. Now, instead, the traffic in Place du 7 Novembre (the date commemorates the 1987 change of government) swirls around an unsmiling clock tower.

Medieval City

The urban sprawl of metropolitan Tunis may leave you cold, but the city's heart beats irresistibly in the medina. Facing modern Tunis, the eastern entry to the medina is the Porte de France, originally Bab el Bahr, meaning the Sea Gate. No matter how rich or important you might be, the only way into the labyrinth from here is on foot.

Enveloped in the medina's fragrance—of spices without name or number, of leather and wool and acrid tobacco smoke—a young salesman may offer you a jasmine posy. Another will try to gain your confidence to guide you to an uncle's shop. The touts and merchants are not too pushy, though you'll rarely escape the invitations, *"Pas cher"* and *"Guten Tag"*, depending on what language they think you speak. Artisans want you to see them at work: the tap-tap of a hammer on a brass tray is part of the come-on. Many are the delights on sale in the maze of souks, from jewellery and carpets to the inevitable knickknacks tourists can scarcely resist, and yet this is not just a show. Food and drink and necessities are sold here. And determinedly non-touristy enterprises offer ancient models of razor blades, rusting bits and pieces from the dawn of the age of electricity, and cigarettes, by the pack or one by one. Browse.

Great Mosque

The streets of the medina are so narrow that the minarets are hidden from view, but you'll hear competing loudspeakers transmitting their muezzin's summons to prayer. The medina's straightest street, Rue Jamma ez-Zitouna, full of the temptations of serious shopping, leads from the Porte de France to the Great Mosque. The Zitouna, or mosque of the Olive Tree, is quite vast considering how it is hemmed in, and more than a thousand years old. It is open to tourists every morning except Friday, when it is jammed with worshippers. Non-Muslims are restricted to a viewing area overlooking the great courtyard.

Hammouda Pasha Mosque

A delicately decorated octagonal minaret marks the Mosque of Hammouda Pasha, a 17th-century landmark. The pasha's father was a convert to Islam, and this mosque is different from all the contemporary buildings, more Italianate than Tunisian.

In the surrounding streets, several palaces and houses have been converted into attractive cafés, restaurants and hotels.

Musée des Arts et Traditions populaires

Lost in the medina, just off Rue des Teinturiers (dyers' street), is a splendid 18th-century palace with a marble courtyard, Dar Ben Abdallah. It houses the city's Museum of Arts and Traditions. Many rooms display the intricate costumes and accessories of the upperclass life of 19th-century Tunis. One section details the transactions and preparations leading up to the wedding of a daughter of the house; others deal with family life and baby care.

Tourbet el Bey

Bustling rue Tourbet el Bey is named after the *tourbet* (mausoleum) at number 62, built in lavish 18th-century style. It offers a crash course in funerary architecture. The tombs of the Husseinite princes crammed in here are marked by carved turbans or, for the more recently deceased, fezzes. Womens' tombs have no hats at all, just marble plaques at either end. The royals who died young are buried in a separate section, behind a carved screen.

Bardo Museum

It's just not fair. At every archaeological site or local museum in Tunisia, you'll hear the same

complaint: "Of course, the best of our finds went to the Bardo." The Musée national du Bardo, in a 19th-century palace on the west side of Tunis, has, indeed, creamed off the indispensable highlights of many centuries of the nation's culture. The irreplaceable collection fills scores of rooms in a palace fit for a king—or in this case a Bey—and there's plenty more stored away in the cellars. (Closed Mondays.)

Bardo's Beginnings

The Roman era takes the lion's share of space—and admiration—at the Bardo, but the story begins many thousands of years earlier. A mystifying but inspiring exhibit, an array of polished stones and bone fragments, was unearthed at a spring in El Guettar, near Gafsa. This Paleolithic monument, dedicated to the spirit of the water source, may be as old as any "religious" monument on earth.

The Phoenician department is full of charming figurines and jewellery, but a stele (an upright stone monument) reminds us of the dark side of Carthage: notice the engraved picture of a priest carrying a baby to be sacrificed.

Neither carpets nor tapestries, but the Roman mosaics of the Bardo Museum.

The Romans

The Bardo claims the world's largest collection of mosaics, so many that visitors tramp over illustrated floors that elsewhere would be under glass. The mosaics from Roman Africa cover themes as pictorial as the hunt, fishing, farming, sailing and sagas of adventure, including the famous version of Ulysses and the Sirens. Accurate pictures of animals are everywhere, some as exotic as ostriches or female centaurs, along with a certain amount of cheerfully erotic subject matter. And there are gigantic Roman statues, most of them with one or another detail mutilated during Vandal incursions.

Finally, the Islamic Department testifies to artistic talent of more recent vintage, starting with rare 10th-century ceramics and calligraphy.

Carthage

For the Phoenicians, the site was special: a defensible North African promontory scarcely a hundred miles from Sicily. The Carthage colony was founded in or around 814 BC and it reached greatness twice, under the Carthaginians and the Romans. Between times, and afterwards, the destruction could scarcely have been more brutal—Carthage was always well supplied with enemies. Plenty is left, though; there's 17 enough work for armies of archaeologists, and you never know what will be uncovered tomorrow.

National Museum of Carthage

On Byrsa hill, overlooking all of Carthage, a modern museum (open daily) sparks the imagination with an uncrowded selection of prize exhibits on the life and art of the ancient colony. The National Museum of Carthage, in a tasteful, airy building, has everything from emotion-charged tomb sculptures to funny-faced, bug-eyed characters portrayed in Punic glass amulets. Explanatory signs are presented in Arabic, French, and (unusually) English.

Cathedral

Next door to the museum, the extravagantly designed St Louis Cathedral is dedicated to the 13th-century French saint/king who died here on the last of the crusades. It is now a cultural centre and is home to the Octobre Musical festival.

The Punic Ports

From Byrsa hill you can look down on the civil and military harbours of ancient Carthage. Archaeologists discovered a sophisticated fortified marina in the military lagoon; the design would probably still work well for submarine pens or a busy ferry station. Nearby is a small oceanographic museum.

The Tophet

Just to the south, the Tophet, or sanctuary, was dedicated to the Punic gods Tanit and Baal Hammon. It looks like an overcrowded graveyard, but the story is even sadder. This is where Carthaginian priests conducted the sacrificial ceremonies in which children were burned to death to appease the gods. Digs

TAKE THE TGM

The archaeological sites of Carthage are interspersed with lavishly gardened modern villas that would be the envy of any Mediterranean seaside suburb or vacation town. (The nicest villa of them all is the seafront presidential palace, guarded by brightly costumed sentries.) A cheap, efficient way to get from Tunis to Carthage, and from one site to another once there, is the TGM, a fast and pleasant commuter railway. The suburban stations, with evocative names like Salammbô and Hannibal, are painted white and blue, with horseshoe arches trimmed with tiles; some platforms are decorated with chunks of ancient columns and capitals.

here have exposed layer upon layer of sarcophagi containing the ashes of children.

Antonine Baths

The most impressive remains of Roman Carthage are along the Mediterranean near the presidential palace. Emperor Antoninus reigned when this vast complex of baths, the biggest in Africa, was opened for business in the 2nd century AD. Only the basement level survived. Surrounding the baths is an archaeological park, a miscellany of ruins enlivened by the conspiratorial spiels of hawkers offering to sell visitors ancient-looking counterfeits.

Sidi Bou Saïd

North of Carthage, the TGM light railway goes to Sidi Bou Saïd, a picture-postcard village of sparkling white houses and cobbled streets perched above the Mediterranean. From the top of the town, seizing views reveal the beauty and expanse of the Bay of Tunis. You might feel an intruder, breaking the peace of the car-free main street, even if it's usually seething with tourists, souvenir salesmen and guides for hire. The film-manufacturing industry rejoices to the nonstop whine of all those cameras recording the whitewashed walls, sky-blue doors, curlicued window grills, purple bougainvillaea and the yacht harbour far below. The rigorous colour scheme, the town's trademark, was codified by Baron Erlanger, whose home, Nejma Ezzahra, has been converted into a Music Museum. In the centre of the village are the mosque and *zaouia* (shrine) of a revered 13th-century sufi, Abu Said Kalafa, after whom it is named.

THE TWO BEST OASES In the desert, even the shade of a single palm tree is a blessing. If it's an infinity of trees straddling gurgling brooks, it's an oasis. The Tunisian desert is well supplied with oases, and two of the most impressive can be reached without benefit of camel or four-wheel-drive transport. In the middle of **Nefta** thousands of palms fill a natural bowl, the Corbeille, and beyond the town is a vast palm grove. On the edges of **Tozeur**, an altogether more charming town, hundreds of thousands of palm trees grow in plantations worth a visit. Make a date.

This is the Coral Coast, backed by the rolling fertile plains of Green Tunisia, the breadbasket of the Roman empire. The north coast, once a lair of the Barbary pirates, is drastically less developed than Tunisia's beachy eastern shores. This is the place for scuba diving, sailing and archaeology. Inland, the scenery will remind you of somewhere warm in Europe; but here Berber women lug firewood on their backs, or herd sheep, goat and cattle miles from anywhere, and donkeys plough the barley fields when the tractors are too busy.

Bizerte

Since time immemorial Bizerte has been coveted for its potential as a naval base. Even before the Romans gave it the unfortunate name of Hyppo-Diarrhytus, it served the Phoenicians as an important Mediterranean outpost. Other rulers, from Vandals to Turks, followed, but it was the French who created a world-class naval installation. The Germans seized it in World War II, whereupon the Allies repeatedly bombed the city. After the war the French returned, overstaying their welcome until 1963, an uncomfortably long time after Tunisian independence was won.

The Old Port

Bizerte's beaches make a pretty picture but the most charming part of the city is the Old Port area, where the fishermen carry on as they always have done, in the shadow of the medina and the kasbah. The houses, whitewashed except for light blue details, come right down to the wide waterfront, as on a Greek island. The difference here is the ochre walls of the kasbah, or fortress, and the sight of a minaret next to the fish market.

The Medina

In the medina, the 17th-century heart of Bizerte, the artisans and tradesmen, from blacksmiths to woodcarvers, still hold forth in their cramped workshops, and the Great Mosque, near the port, is the focus of religious and architectural interest. The kasbah, just to the east, is a maze fraught with mystery but minus any menace. The locals seem delighted to discover tourists on their doorstep, and if you get lost, a child or two will cheerfully lead you back to a street wide enough for cars. The Spanish Fort on the

The pace is as calm as the sea in the old harbour of Bizerte.

hilltop northwest of the medina is actually misnamed; it was built by the Turks in the 16th century.

Modern Bizerte

Sparkling white buildings, palm trees, parks and beaches give a spacious air to the modern city. The Route de la Corniche heads north to an inviting area of extensive white beaches, on which a few comfortable hotels have been built. Collectors of superlatives will want to keep going as far as windy Cap Blanc, claiming to be the northernmost point on the African continent.

Tabarka

Like Bizerte, Tabarka, at the far western end of the north coast, was a Phoenician trading post. Now the traders are trying to sell you coral jewellery and rugs, for Tabarka has become a serious tourist centre. The infrastructure includes an international airport, a yacht harbour surrounded by cosy modern villas, a dramatically sited seaside golf course and a stylish complex of hotels and holiday flats.

The Castle

From the oak- and pine-covered hills that descend to the seaside there's an imposing view of a historic castle on an island in the harbour. A French-built causeway runs from the port to the isle, compromising its insularity, but the mood is inescapable. Called the Genoese fortress, the castle was owned from the 16th to 18th centuries by a family of merchants from Genoa. How the Lomellini family came to the castle is the final chapter of a Barbary coast saga. After the influential pirate Dragut was captured and enslaved by the Genoese, his liberation was negotiated through Emperor Charles V of Spain, in exchange for the island. Today the castle is unoccupied but for a working lighthouse.

THE THREE BEST MEDINAS Many a Tunisian city has an old town of memorable charm, but here are three nominations for truly unforgettable ones. **Kairouan**: Yes, you can get lost; no, you'll never be bored; and wonders are on sale. **Sousse**: An enormous walled city of historic monuments and real life. **Tunis**: All the intrigue, animation and fragrance of yore just beyond the modern capital city.

Les Aiguilles

Just beyond the town centre, a geological formation called "the Needles" is a favourite spot for a stroll. Lining the shore are pinnacles that look like Disneyesque sandcastles with cracks in them. Offshore, the fields of coral and the marine life make this coast an eyeful for scuba divers.

Aïn Draham

Escapees from the heat of a Tunisian summer head for this Alpine-style resort in the midst of cork forests. It's cool and fragrant and a base for winter hunting trips. (Wild boar is the target, and it often winds up on local menus.) With its red-roofed chalet architecture, a relic of the French era, Aïn Draham couldn't be confused with any other town.

Hammam Bourguiba

Closer to the Algerian border, the thermal station of Hammam Bourguiba enjoys a mild, dry valley setting. One of the three most important health spas in the country, it specializes in treatment for respiratory problems. The Romans were the first to appreciate its sulphur springs.

Dougga

Nowhere is Roman Africa more admirably arrayed than at Dougga, within day-trip distance of Tabarka or Tunis. The ruins of

---

LANDLOCKED UTICA

Whatever became of Utica, founded in 1100 BC as the first Phoenician colony in Africa? Today it's an obscure turn-off on the road from Tunis to Bizerte. Silting has stranded the historic port 12 km (7 miles) from the sea, and in general time has been unkind. The ruins of the Roman city, not terribly extensive, are there as a reminder, and a small museum fills in some of the gaps.

---

this elegant city are well cared for but uncommercialized, except for a few guides and postcard sellers.

Dougga's apogee came in the 2nd and 3rd centuries AD. Then, while other parts of the Roman empire were embracing Christianity, the conservative folk of Dougga held on to the familiar pagan gods. By the 6th century the city had lost its role; but it was still inhabited as late as the mid-20th century. A far less desirable site down the hill was decreed for the construction of Nouvelle Dougga, to which the residents were displaced to make way for the archaeologists.

Roman Theatre

The Romans usually chose flat terrain for their logical urban plans, but here they found a way

23

to exploit a magical hillslope site already chosen by the ancient Numidians. From the cheap seats in the Roman theatre, built into the bowl of the hillside, the view beyond the stage goes on for miles of green. Small by Roman standards, the theatre has been partly restored so that modern drama-lovers can approximate the experience at festival times.

The Capitol

An outstanding tribute to ancient Roman engineering, architecture and sculpture, the Capitol is roofless but otherwise largely unscathed. Four Corinthian columns support a pediment showing its age with jagged edges and windblown inscription. The temple is the more breathtaking for its golden Dougga stone.

Temples and More

Temples to Minerva, Saturn, Juno, Pluto and other gods brood in various stages of ruin. Evocative, too, are the Plaza of Winds, with a 12-point compass incised in the paving, and the old marketplace. Fine mosaics have been uncovered all but intact, and left in place. Down the hillside on the south side of town the archaeologists discovered a bath-house, a large public convenience, and a brothel now called the House of the Trefoil. Farther south, the Libyan-Punic Mausoleum rises above the olive trees. A precocious impression of a belfry, it looks out of place among the classical ruins, but predates them.

Bulla Regia

Set in rich agricultural country framed by velvet hillsides, Bulla Regia was an important Roman city with all contemporary comforts plus an astonishing exclusivity: underground villas in which the rich and powerful could escape the heat of summer. The best of the sculptures from Bulla Regia were moved to the Bardo Museum in Tunis, but many memorable mosaics were left where they were found.

The site is something of a maze; you rarely know what you'll find around a corner. Look for the partly restored Roman Theatre, the baths, the Capitol, the Forum and the market, and two Christian basilicas. But the villas, so carefully designed and executed, are the high spot.

Chemtou Museum

Across the road from the archaeological site, a small museum (where Bulla Regia entry tickets are sold) features statues and stone carvings that escaped the talent scouts from the Bardo. There is a small bookshop and a café, as well. You can sit beneath a bottlebrush tree amongst the white irises and geraniums.

25

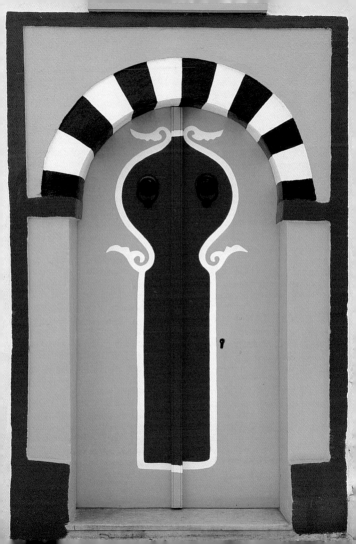

CAP BON
Kerkouane, Kelibia, Korbous, Nabeul, Hammamet

On the shores of the Cap Bon peninsula, the beaches are tremendous—and so is the development of tourism. Still, there's room for all, and the fishermen go about their business as ever, and the orange groves and vineyards rarely see a delegation from the coastal throngs. Fertile Cap Bon, a finger pointing at Sicily, is mostly a flat, out-on-a-limb sort of place, a long way from any African clichés—until you spot a camel pulling a plough.

Kerkouane

On a bluff overlooking the Mediterranean, archaeologists made a stunning discovery in 1952: a big Carthaginian village that had lain abandoned for more than 2,000 years. Unlike the Punic capital, Carthage, Kerkouane was left to rest undisturbed in oblivion; no conqueror came to recycle its stones. Archaeologists have left the walls knee-high or lower, though abundant cement has been used to re-create even that much. The street plan is evident, as is the design of the houses, notable for the plumbing and the

Family life is kept well out of public view, behind elegantly decorated doors.

shallow baths. (The Romans were gregarious in their ablutions but the Carthaginians seem to have bathed at home.) Between the archaeological site and the white museum building is a formal flower-and-herb garden.

The Museum

A careful selection of jewellery, statuary and pottery is on show at the Kerkouane museum. One of its prized treasures is a wooden sarcophagus cover carved in the form of the goddess Astarte and known as the "Princess of Kerkouane". Among novelties are a bronze razor with a swan's-head handle and an early version of gamblers' dice, both exhibits from the 4th to 3rd centuries BC. And there are those charming Punic heads with goggle eyes and ringlet beards. (The site and the museum are closed Mondays.)

Kelibia

From miles away you can see the silhouette of the 6th-century fortress of Kelibia, a vision rising from the coastline like the top of the head of a behemoth with a brush haircut. A rugged unpaved road leads up to the entrance of the castle, still inhabited by some soldiers and a handful of civilians, and visitable.

Archaeologically, everything inside the fort is in an early stage of investigation except for the fully restored crenellated wall encircling the installation. Interesting relics haphazardly arrayed represent eras from ancient Rome to World War II. Historic cannon from various armies poke through holes in the wall.

The fort dominates the coast, so the views from the battlements provide a good perspective on the low-key resort areas nearby.

Korbous

Since the days of the Romans, who called it Aquæ Calidæ Carpitanæ, Korbous has been a spa. It occupies a narrow Cap Bon valley facing the Gulf of Tunis. Seven different springs, each with its own special values, keep the enthusiasts drinking and bathing. Here they claim to cure problems ranging from rheumatism to nerves to dental complications.

But you don't have to be ill: they welcome healthy people, too.

A few kilometres beyond Korbous, the mineral spring of Aïn Oktor delivers cold water which the *curistes* drink, in vast quantities, to deal with problems like kidney stones. Otherwise, it's a matter of taste.

Nabeul

In the middle of the main intersection a potted araucaria pine tree proclaims Nabeul's vocation: pots. Actually, the cheerfully decorated, gigantic Ali Baba pot was cleverly built around the base of the tree, but makes a startling landmark. Thanks to the high quality of the region's clay,

Nabeul produces pottery in all shapes and sizes.

ceramics of all sorts are the backbone of the local handicrafts industry. No wonder this is a vital stop for souvenir shoppers.

The administrative capital of Cap Bon, Nabeul is a splendid town for strolling at leisure. It is packed full of irresistible temptations. In addition to pottery of every imaginable form there are local specialities such as embroidery, lace and home-made perfumes. One strong influence on Nabeul ceramics: Muslim refugees who came here from Andalusia after the Christian Reconquest, bringing their skills and intricate designs for *azulejos*, decorated tiles. For another slant on shopping, try Nabeul's weekly market, held every Friday, where they sell everything from secondhand clothes to full-grown camels.

Archaeology Museum

Well-tended gardens bright with geraniums, hibiscus and roses fill the courtyard leading to Nabeul's museum. As in other Tunisian museums, the ancient mosaics are of the highest quality; some here have rather racy subject matter. Also of interest are the Punic sculptures, charms and artefacts, and Roman ceramics. The museum is closed Mondays. The Roman town of Neapolis, southwest of Nabeul, is still being excavated.

Hammamet

Big-time international tourism, Tunisian style, reaches its climax in Hammamet, the bull's-eye of beaches, hotels, thalassotherapy centres, golf courses and entertainment. It was inevitable, since this is the country's only south-facing beach, attached to a most agreeable town. Making the most of the resort's success with a seemingly endless extension of the hotel zone, they have yet to run out of sand that's fine, clean and desirable.

You'd think the great sweeping Gulf of Hammamet would have inspired real estate developers since Roman times, but it wasn't "discovered" until the 1920s. Then a Romanian millionaire named Georges Sebastian built a sumptuous villa, inspiring other foreigners to share the North African dream. It's been years since anyone came here for the peace and quiet, but the names include Flaubert, Gide, Klee and Wilde. Sebastian's residence has been transformed into the International Cultural Centre, while other villas have been incorporated into larger hotels.

The Medina

Hammamet's old walled town comes right down to the beach, where fishing boats sit high and dry between outings. Just inside 29

Sun-worshippers find a dream of a beach in Hammamet.

the walls are tourist bazaars wheeling and dealing in souvenirs, but beyond the hurly-burly is an authentic whiff of traditional Hammamet—lived-in old houses lining narrow lanes, their whitewashed walls adorned with good-luck signs of fishes and Hands of Fatima. The views from the much-restored battlements are full of happy surprises, down onto enviable white houses with roof gardens and out to the beach and the sea.

Market Day

If Hammamet seems too touristical, stick around until Thursday. The weekly market, which fills streets at the top of Avenue de la République, spreading into the fields northeast of the town centre, is the real thing. (It actually starts on Wednesday evening on a smaller scale.) Spread out in the hot sun are shiny arrays of enticing fruit and vegetables—go easy on those dangerous-looking hot peppers. Amongst displays of pots and pans, plastic junk, cosmetics and used shoes, a few mild-mannered beggars hope for a handout.

Yasmine Hammamet

This new resort has many hotels and restaurants, a fine marina and charming medina.

▶ THE SAHEL

Sousse, Port El Kantaoui, Monastir, El Djem,
Kairouan, Sbeitla, Mahdia, Sfax, Kerkennah Islands

Never to be confused with West Africa's parched Sahel region, the Tunisian Sahel (meaning "coast") is rich in resources and beauty. Millions of olive trees—more than you would believe—stretch in endless ranks. The coast itself, one fine beach after another, performs an expanding tourist mission but the exploitation is more restrained than the typical European *Costa*. And inland excursions offer sensational experiences, from the Roman amphitheatre of El Djem to the pilgrim city of Kairouan.

Sousse

Perfect beaches, a hard-working port and an old walled town reeking with tradition coincide at Sousse. After a day or two you'll get used to the incongruities of this hub of trains, ships, horse-drawn carriages and cargo-carrying donkeys, just as local ladies all wrapped up in their *haiks* inscrutably view the semi-nudity of pink tourists sunbathing on the strand. The city goes back to Phoenician days; in fact, it may well have been founded nearly 3,000 years ago, even before Carthage.

Under the ancient Romans it thrived until the 3rd century AD.

Vandals and Byzantines followed, but most of what makes Sousse fascinating dates from the 9th century, when it was a vital port of the Aghlabid empire. (From Sousse, Arab invaders sailed to subdue Sicily.)

The Medina

A lively mixture of history, commerce and faith, the Sousse medina is home to tens of thousands of people. It is impressively walled, except for a gap facing the port, the target of Allied bombardment in World War II. The medina rises from the port area to the kasbah at the top of the hill, too much to tackle in a single incursion. High above the ramparts and the minarets within, a lighthouse, the Khalef Tower, was erected in AD 859. You can climb to the top for the all-encompassing view. At ground level in the medina you can hardly avoid the shopping temptations among the stimulating sights, sounds and smells of the souks.

The Ribat

To reach the front door of this 8th-century fortified monastery, which has subsided below the level of the rest of the medina, 31

In the Sousse medina, fortress-like walls surround the Great Mosque.

you have to go down stairs; the city grew upwards, around its oldest monument. You can visit the halls where the Islamic warrior monks trained and prayed, and the cells they lived in. (The *murabitin* were something like the Muslim equivalent of Crusaders.) A spiral staircase goes to the top of the lookout and signal tower, for a monk's-eye perspective of the medina.

Great Mosque

Horseshoe arches surround the stately courtyard of the Great Mosque, built in AD 850. Visitors with tickets from the tourist office can penetrate the fortress-like walls and enter the courtyard, paved in marble that shines in the sunlight, between 9 a.m. and 1 p.m. daily except during Friday prayers. But the prayer hall is out of bounds to non-Muslims.

Sousse Museum

At the very top of the walled city, at the southwest corner of the kasbah, the Sousse Museum contains a collection of Roman mosaics fit for a Caesar. Created between the 1st and 6th centuries, and illustrating themes religious, mythological and simply picturesque or lusty, they are well displayed in a rambling layout with a refreshing garden in its midst. In terms of quality if not quantity, these mosaics are a serious challenge to the Bardo museum. By way of three-dimensional distraction, the museum also shows funerary sculptures from the Punic to the Christian eras.

Port El Kantaoui

The style of architecture at Port El Kantaoui, Tunisia's first planned tourism centre, is described as Turkish-Arabic and Andalusian. Whatever you call it, this is a startling seaside mirage, all white, surrounding a 300-yacht marina full of dream-boats arrived from Bremen and Seattle, Hull and La Rochelle. Extending along the beaches beyond the marina are many hotels including several luxurious five-star complexes.

From the landward side you enter Port El Kantaoui through a simulated historic gate, leading to an ideal traffic-free world of low-rise holiday apartments, shops, restaurants, cafés, and unhurried browsing. Sports possibilities range from swimming and boating to golf—a 27-hole course between the olive groves and the sea. On the beaches, camels with devastatingly flirtatious eyelashes are available for photo opportunities or trekking.

Monastir

For the Phoenicians the harbour was a natural, and this became one of their trading posts, named Rous. The Romans called it Ruspina. In the 8th century, the Aghlabid dynasty built the town's military and spiritual force.

And then Habib Bourguiba was born here in 1903, and as his political star brightened so did the town's economy. By the time the president-for-life was deposed in 1987, and installed in his home-town retirement palace, Monastir's infrastructure was already highly developed, its historic monuments well restored, new ones built, and the tourism business—hotels, marina complex and golf—was booming.

The Mausoleum

The town's most amazing building is the Bourguiba Mausoleum, 33 a stupendous twin-towered, gold-domed memorial complex more lavish than most emperors could imagine. It was completed in the 1970s in long-range anticipation of the president's funereal needs. Not far away, honouring Bourguiba, stands an astonishing gilt statue of an earnest youth. On the edge of the medina, the Bourguiba Mosque is a modern recapitulation of various Islamic architectural forms. The medina itself is unlike typical old towns in Tunisia; the streets follow a grid pattern, with arcades providing shade for souvenir shoppers.

The Ribat

Overlooking the Mediterranean, its severe walls refurbished like new, Monastir's ribat was begun in the 8th century. Here the warrior-monks of Islam gathered to pray, defend the city, and mobilize for raids on infidels overseas. It all looks so authentically old and Arabic that it's a favourite location for foreign film companies staging biblical extravaganzas. The original prayer hall now serves as a museum of Islamic art, well stocked with exhibitions of classical calligraphy, jewellery, pottery and even figurative art.

El Djem

A road veering off the eucalyptus-lined main highway from Sousse to Sfax heads straight as an arrow toward an amazing apparition. Discovering one of the Roman Empire's biggest colosseums in the middle of an infinity of olive trees is guaranteed to wake any drowsy traveller.

El Djem (or El Jem) used to be called Thysdrus. It was known as a farming centre in Carthaginian days, but nothing very memorable occurred until the 3rd century AD when the Romans chose this site to build Africa's biggest amphitheatre. But Thysdrus bet on the wrong politician in an uprising, so the Roman Legionnaires inflicted punishment in the fashion of the time, sacking the town. Thereafter the colosseum languished or served as a fortress or a mere marketplace. In modern times, appreciation of ancient monuments put El Djem back on the map, and it is sometimes used for musical and dramatic spectacles.

The Amphitheatre

Look through the arches upon arches toward the sky; the architectural and engineering genius is open to your admiration. In its heyday 30,000 fans of life-and-death spectacles—men against animals, animals against animals, and men against men—were seated around the elliptical amphitheatre.

Apart from normal wear and tear, the colosseum was involved

in several battles and partially dismantled by cannon fire in the middle of the 19th century. More than enough is left to whet the imagination.

Archaeological Museum

Built around a patio filled with flourishing banana plants, El Djem's museum has a remarkable collection of Roman mosaics that the Bardo neglected to appropriate. There are delicately featured portraits of mythological characters, and animals, and abstractions.

Some fine mosaics can be viewed *in situ* just outside the museum, where archaeologists are still unearthing the old town's shops and houses.

Kairouan

This holiest of North African cities packs in the pilgrims, but it's not all solemn and spiritual. Kairouan's medina is as lively as an Arabian Nights circus, and the people—surprisingly resilient to the tourist onslaught—manage to stay friendly. The sacred side of the city is deeply impressive; the secular, particularly the gift shopping, will leave you smiling.

Kairouan was founded around 670 by the conqueror Oqba ibn Nafi, a companion of the prophet Mohammed himself. The site was hot and unappealing, but that was an advantage in the search

for a place unsullied by infidels, meant to become "a rampart for Islam until the end of the world". Unfortunately for Kairouan's defenders, the citadel was overrun by a heretical sect of Berbers in 757. But it eventually recovered, and under the Aghlabids became a centre of faith and scholarship. Kairouan is usually rated fourth among the holiest cities of Islam, behind Mecca, Medina and Jerusalem. They say that if you can't make it to Mecca, seven pilgrimages to Kairouan are just as effective.

The Great Mosque

Regardless of your religious inclinations or disinclinations, the indisputable grandeur permeating the Great Mosque focuses the spirit. In spite of the crowds, peace prevails in the parade-ground-sized courtyard, marble-paved, surrounded by the Muslim equivalent of a cloister. The pillars, relics of ancient civilizations starting with Carthaginian, support Islamic horseshoe arches. Non-believers are barred from the cool, dark prayer hall, but you can peer through the windows at the rich tiles and calligraphy and the sparrows flitting among the arches and the great chandeliers. This was the site of the first mosque in North Africa; the present building was begun in the 9th century. The base of the powerful, 35

three-storey minaret is said to predate this; note the optical illusion designed to harmonize the apparent size of the windows.

Mosque of the Barber

Your ticket to the Great Mosque is also valid for the Zaouia of Sidi Sahab, known as the Mosque of the Barber. This is the burial place of Abu Zama el Belaoui, a companion and disciple of the prophet Mohammed. He zealously guarded three hairs from the Prophet's beard, hence the "barber" reference. This is an important place of pilgrimage, and yet the courtyard provides relaxing escape from the sun and hubbub outside.

Water Projects

Next to the tourist office, the Aghlabid Pools are a wildly ambitious, thousand-year-old project to provide a dependable water supply to dry and dusty Kairouan. An aqueduct brought water from rain-prone hills to this vast storage area.

Another odd element in the water supply situation: the Bir Barouta in the middle of the medina is a well that legend credits with supplying a specially

Sheltered by ochre battlements, Kairouan is the holiest of North African cities.

JUST THE TICKET

The Tourist Office on the edge of the old town, in Avenue de la République, delivers tickets valid for three monuments: the Great Mosque; the Zaouia of Sidi Sahab (the Barber), one of Mohammed's companions; and the Zaouia of Sidi Amor Abbada. At the entrance to the Great Mosque a doorman assigns a white smock to anyone, male or female, wearing shorts or otherwise inappropriate garb. When you return the smock on the way out, a tip is appreciated.

holy sort of water. The pumping is done by a blindfolded camel walking in circles.

The Medina

There are no disappointments in the medina of Kairouan, a maze so colourful your imagination will tingle. The deeper you go into the shadowy world beyond the souvenir hustlers near the main gate the more intriguing it all becomes. Kairouan is renowned for its carpets; the industry employs a sizeable percentage of the population, and in many a patio you'll glimpse a work in progress. On another plane, a distinguished local speciality is a sweet called *makroudh*, a little

diamond-shaped cake filled with date paste and dripping with honey syrup. Mounds of them are being cooked up all day in the souks, to be doled out into small plastic bags, bought for a pittance and eaten, stickily, on the run or at home.

Sbeitla

About 100 km (more than 60 miles) southwest of Kairouan, rich archaeological pickings adjoin the nondescript modern town of Sbeitla. Dispersed in the sunshine, temples, churches and a triumphal arch mark the long-abandoned city of Sufetula, a heroic footnote to the declining days of the Roman empire.

The Forum dates from the 2nd century AD. The dramatic turning point came in the 7th century, when Gregorius, the patriarch and governor of the province, defied the Byzantine empire and moved his capital from Carthage to Sufetula. Constantinople was too far away to exact any reprisals but the secessionists soon succumbed to an Arab invasion. The self-styled emperor was slain, and Sufetela was levelled and forgotten for more than a thousand years.

From dried rose petals to ground coriander, a wide selection of spices for your personal blend.

On the Site

The triumphal arch of Sufetula was built under the reign of Diocletian at the end of the 3rd century. Three pagan temples and several Christian churches sum up the spiritual evolution of the town. The temples are believed to be dedicated to Jupiter, Juno and Minerva, an unusual and extravagant gesture, since most Roman cities had a single temple shared by all three. Two of the churches were Catholic, a third—the church of Servus—is thought to have belonged to a schismatic North African sect, the Donatists. Otherwise, the archaeological zone is full of the elements of a typical Roman city—markets, public and private baths, the forum and the theatre. It's all especially evocative at sunset.

Mahdia

On the coast south of Monastir, Mahdia is a real working port, a relaxed, unspoiled town. Big trawlers congregate in a modern harbour, where sailors stretch out their enormous nets in the shade for inspection and maintenance. By no coincidence, some sumptuous seafood is served nearby, at remarkably low prices.

Mahdia has a spirited history. In the 10th century it became the capital of the Fatimid dynasty, who claimed to be descendants of

Fatima, the daughter of the Prophet. They were vehemently opposed by orthodox Muslims, so the defensive potential of Mahdia's peninsula was an appealing site. In succeeding centuries other Islamic sects as well as Christians fought over the town. Among colourful invaders were the English, French and Spanish.

The Medina

An impressive tunnel entrance leads through fortifications separating the new town from the medina. The Skifa el Kahla gate was rebuilt after Spanish troops blew it up in the middle of the 16th century. A few salesmen now haunt the dark passage. The medina's most imposing building, the Great Mosque, is a modern reconstruction of a thousand-year-old landmark; apparently there never was a minaret.

Farther down the peninsula, beyond the Borj el Kebir fortress, the city narrows to a windswept promontory with a lighthouse. Offshore here, at the beginning of the 20th century, Mahdia sponge fishermen discovered the wreck of a Roman galley jammed with bronze and marble statues and other works of art.

Sfax

Though it's alongside the Mediterranean, Tunisia's second-biggest city is essentially beachless, so it has escaped the upheavals of tourism. The citizens of Sfax, long known for their commercial dynamism, take their prosperity from other sources—minerals, olives, almonds and manufactured goods exported through the big modern port.

On three sides, Sfax is surrounded by millions of olive trees, separated from the heart of the city by so much urban sprawl that you may think you'll never reach the centre. But it's well worth persevering, for the medina is a winner, and the modern, tree-

4

THE FOUR BEST BEACHES Sunbathers, swimmers snorkellers and scuba divers are all looking for something different in beaches, so any choice is subjective. Here are four of the best. **Hammamet**: long and lovely, and the sun is in the right place. **Isle of Djerba**: supremely white, powdery and endlessly uncrowded. **Raf Raf**: dramatically beautiful, isolated setting; and what a nice name! **Kelibia**: Tunisians' choice for a family getaway.

lined centre of the city is considered the most elegant in the country.

Modern City

The area from the old town to the harbour is airy, bright and sparkling—thanks mostly to World War II. During the war Sfax was an Axis base, hence the target of most intense Allied bombing and shelling.

When it was all over—Free French and British troops captured the city early in 1943—there were many empty spaces appropriate for parks, squares and boulevards, and the port had to be rebuilt from zero. The new town's architectural style, a colonial version of Moorish traditions, makes good use of horseshoe arches and coloured tiles.

Archaeological Museum

The City Hall is a rather disquieting compromise between European and Arabian architectural styles: it has a French clock tower that reaches a minaret-like pinnacle, as well as a great central dome looming above a crenellated wall. Inside, on the ground floor, the Archaeological Museum offers a good briefing on the history of Sfax, which the ancient Romans called Taparura. The exhibits range from Roman funerary urns and coins to Byzantine mosaics.

The Medina

Getting lost within the 9th-century ramparts of the Sfax medina is considerably less of a problem than in, say, Tunis. Many of the residential and shopping streets are logically laid out and wide enough for sunshine to penetrate. The old town has a convincingly authentic air, no doubt due to the almost total absence of tourist-oriented souvenir stalls. The souks are full of enticements, though—carpets, fabrics, jewellery and spices. If there is a disappointment, it must be the kasbah, which, after 11 centuries of varied uses, has been converted into a small outdoor theatre.

Dar Jallouli Museum

This outstanding museum of traditional costumes and popular arts occupies a beautiful 17th-century town house in the medina, where Rue de la Driba and Rue Sidi Ali Ennouri meet. In the rooms set around a paved interiour courtyard you can see costumes of tremendously rich material and colour, plus everything revealing of local life from carved or painted furniture to household implements, jewellery and calligraphy.

Kerkennah Islands

Among the exports transiting the busy port of Sfax are tourists. Six times a day in summer a ferry leaves on the one-hour trip to the Kerkennah Islands, a favourite destination for sun-lovers who want to stick close to the beach. For undistracted escapism, it's hard to beat these palmy Mediterranean isles barely keeping their heads above sea level, best explored by bicycle.

The Phoenicians got here first, and Hannibal sought refuge in Kerkennah to avoid some unpleasantness in Carthage in 195 BC. Over the centuries local fishermen had to put up with waves of raiders—Vikings, Sicilians, Spaniards and crusaders. In spite of everything, the islanders remain uncommonly hospitable.

On the Archipelago

The ferryboats from Sfax go to Sidi Youssef on the western end of the westernmost isle, Gharbi, also called Melita after the main village. Gharbi (meaning "western") is connected to the other main island, Chergui ("eastern") by El Kantara, a causeway attributed to the ancient Romans. The centre of touristic interest on the beachy north coast of Chergui, is a low-key, low-rise hotel zone in the Sidi Frej area. You can walk along a coastal path to Borj el Hissar, a fort built on the site of an old Roman settlement. Beyond Sidi Frej in Remla, the main town of the archipelago, the amenities range from a bank to a couple of pharmacies. A dirt road leads to Sidi Fankhal beach.

Activities on the isles are geared to the sea—swimming, sailing, windsurfing, and accompanying local fishermen on their unique brand of fish harvest. Ashore you can go horse riding, play tennis, ride a camel and watch folklore shows.

Chergui is the perfect isle for lazing around and recharging your batteries.

Sand roasting in the sun, stretching to the Saharan horizon or fringing the Mediterranean with an invitation, sets southern Tunisia's moods. Get set for startling images: of camels ambling along a beach, of mirages and oases and people who beat the heat as cave-dwellers. For conciseness this chapter lumps together regions covering roughly the southern half of Tunisia, starting with the country's most popular island. People have been falling in love with its simple beauty since the time of the ancient Greeks.

Isle of Djerba

Homer is credited with immortalizing Djerba—well, maybe it was Djerba—as the Lotus-Eaters' Isle. In the *Odyssey*, he tells of the sailors of Ulysses so charmed by their island layover that they had to be chained to get them back on board. After a time along the white, soft, dreamy beaches that all but encircle Djerba you may feel the same way.

Dry as a blotter, but rich in palm and olive trees, Djerba has an area of 514 sq km (198 sq miles), smaller than the Isle of Man, Corfu or Ibiza. Low-slung and inoffensive, yet very highly developed, the tourist zone sprawls out along the northeast quadrant of the coast.

Although it's linked to mainland Tunisia by a causeway, Djerba remains psychologically insular, its traditions unaffected by the surrounding world. Where else in Tunisia would you find women sporting pointed straw hats? The fortified mosques and simple white houses and handicrafts are also distinctive. As is the strict version of the Muslim religion practised by a strong minority of the inhabitants. Unusual, too, is Djerba's small Jewish community, which claims to trace its roots here to the 6th century BC.

Houmt Souk

The island's main town, Houmt Souk, is guarded by a no-nonsense seafront fortress; its severe crenellated walls have seen every kind of war and siege and derring-do.

The medieval Borj el Kebir seems to have been a Roman bastion at the outset. In 1560 its Spanish defenders were besieged for two months by the legendary pirate Dragut on behalf of the Ottoman empire. When Dragut finally surmounted the battlements he showed no mercy. For 43 centuries a pyramid of skulls—5,000, it was said—stood nearby, until the Bey of Tunis ordered it replaced by a less terrifying obelisk.

In the shadow of the fort an outdoor market serves the islanders with the essentials of life, from sumptuous fruits and vegetables to clothing, new and not so new. Souvenir hunters prefer the market in the centre of town, a cornucopia of handicrafts, rugs, jewellery and ceramics. No matter where you're from, you'll quickly discover that these souk super-salesmen speak your language.

More Monuments

Houmt Souk has its quota of the island's 300 or so religious buildings. Typical of the dangerous days of yore, the Zaouia of Sidi Ibrahim Jomni has fortress-like walls.

The all-white Mosque of the Strangers, across the road, is alto-

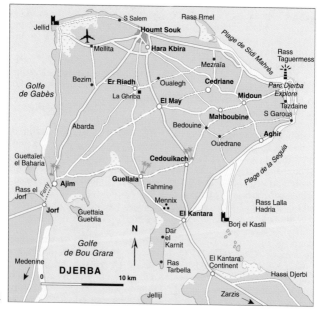

gether more extroverted, with its bubble domes and finely carved minaret.

One 18th-century *zaouia* that is open even to non-believers is now the Museum of Popular Arts and Traditions. This institution displays everything you need to know about Djerban rituals, costumes, handicrafts and everyday life. The rambling building itself is intriguing, especially the formidably decorated interior of the main dome.

Midoun

The second-biggest town on the island, Midoun, is notable for its large population of the descendants of slaves who came this far by caravan across the Sahara. Indeed, the slave trade was one of the foundations of the island's economy until the commerce was abolished in the middle of the 19th century.

The best time to visit Midoun is on Friday, when the weekly market takes over much of the town. Barefoot or in sandals, sellers of frying pans, nail-clippers and flashlight batteries squat or lie behind their displays, roasting in the sun, waiting utterly patiently for fate to send a customer to haggle with. The people here—sellers, buyers, beggars and hangers-on—are a rich cross-section of the brilliant colour of Djerban life.

Parc Djerba Explore

At the foot of Taguermess lighthouse, this theme park is divided into several areas: a traditional Djerba village, with boutiques, cafés and restaurants in various architectural styles; the Lalla Hadria Museum and its superb collection of Tunisian and Arab-Islamic art tracing 13 centuries of art and history; the Djerba Heritage, presenting the island's architecture and way of life, where you can join in activities such as weaving and pottery; and Crocod'iles, a crocodile farm with 400 reptiles in a desert décor.

La Ghriba

Barefoot believers mount a vigil in the synagogue of La Ghriba, reading non-stop in sing-song tones the words of the Torah, or holy scroll. This has been going on here for literally thousands of years. According to local tradition, the synagogue was founded in 586 BC by a band of Jews who escaped from Nebuchadnezzar. In recent years the Jewish community has dwindled with emigration to Israel.

The present building is a gaily decorated early 20th-century fantasy with Moorish arches, geometrically decorated tiles and an intricate ceiling. Visitors of any persuasion are welcome here but they must remove their shoes as 45 in a mosque and cover their heads. Donations are solicited. Across the lane from the synagogue is a *fondouk* or hostel for pilgrims; they come from all over North Africa and Europe for Passover and other occasions.

Guellala

You may never get closer to a working potter than in the village of Guellala, one of Tunisia's leading ceramics centres, near the south coast of the island. The brief main street is lined with ceramics shops, some of which create their products on the premises. Guellala's output is generally rustic, as it has been since the days when it exported big terracotta amphoras to store the oil and water of several countries.

Zarzis

The isle of Djerba is linked to the peninsula of Zarzis by a causeway about 7 km (4 miles) long,

sometimes called the Roman road; others say the Carthaginians first built it. This brilliant engineering project fell into disuse for several centuries until modern times.

The town of Zarzis, a seaside oasis, is surrounded on three sides by endless olive and palm groves. With spacious plazas and roundabouts from the French protectorate era, Zarzis has something of an old colonial style. A few resort hotels have gone up along the beaches north of town, but tourist development is on a small scale by Djerba standards.

Gabès

By road or rail, the port city of Gabès is a key junction between the north and west and the deep south. The ancient Romans gave it the name Tacape. Nowadays it's a curious mixture of industrial and commercial centre, with a small-scale tourist development clinging to its beach in

THE FIVE MOST AMAZING VIEWS You'll gasp with wonder at some of Tunisia's sights, both natural and man-made. **Chott El Jerid**: endless, mystical salt flats, prone to mirages. **El Djem**: the road from nowhere leads straight to a colossal colosseum. **Sidi Bou Saïd**: a white-and-blue village to sigh over. The Sahara at **Douz**: where the dunes begin, and fade into infinity. Troglodytes at **Matmata**: burrowed into hills, to escape the heat.

sight of the chemical plants' smokestacks. The most remarkable feature of all is an oasis that reaches from desert to sea.

North and west of the town stretch hundreds of thousands of palm trees. Horse-drawn carriages (calèches) follow the zigzag of tracks through the palm groves, winding up in the cool Chenini oasis, where there is a small zoo and crocodile-and-alligator farm. The Gabès palm trees provide refreshing shade but the dates growing on them are not of top quality, lacking the perfect desert climate. Still, the dates go down well as animal feed, and the dateless tree trunks are used for making furniture or poles.

Local Colour

The big, friendly Jara Market, on the north side of Gabès, is the place to price wickerwork, rugs, and wonderful, fragrant commodities that come in big sacks: mint, incense, the local henna, dried beans, coriander, peppers, saffron.

On the Avenue de la République, south of town, the Museum of Arts and Popular Traditions occupies a one-time medersa, a school for Koranic scholars. In this stately 17th-century building you can see brilliantly coloured Berber costumes, gold and silver jewellery and widely ranging cultural exhibits.

Matmata

Ingenious desert architecture is the almost-hidden attraction of Matmata, a Berber town about 40 km (25 miles) south of Gabès. On the way, the rocky desert is enlivened by big tufts of brush and, occasionally, clumps of olive and palm trees around minioases. Matmata is surrounded by pink mountains with deep, worried furrows. The secret of the moonscape and the underground housing was spread worldwide in the films Star Wars and Raiders of the Lost Ark.

Matmata's houses are burrowed into the soft clay, keeping them cool in the sweltering summer and warm on cold winter nights. Apartments surround a central patio, dug out like a well, that lets in sun and air, the whole complex virtually invisible from ground level. (After a while, though, you'll begin to notice tell-tale craters with residents popping in and out.) They've been doing it this way for centuries, and several thousand local people are thus sheltered today. There's no end to the underground permutations, as living quarters can lead to a complex of storage rooms, stables, cisterns and granaries.

To sample the troglodytic way of life on a more luxurious plane, you can stay in one of the underground hotels.

47

Kebili

On the long, straight, lonely road from Gabès to the oasis of Kebili you know you're entering a new sort of world. To the north: the salt lake called Chott El Fejej. To the south: scrubby desert leading to the Jebel Tebaga mountain range. And the town itself has the air of a semi-abandoned Foreign Legion outpost. Until the 19th century the big business here was the slave trade.

Every Tuesday is market day for the whole region. A dozen dusty streets of Kebili are lined with sellers of food, clothing, household goods, and cardboard boxes displaying items of indeterminate character: are they pebbles? dried fish? salt crystals? In November Kebili stages a date harvest festival.

Kebili may be unglamorous, but, as always, it's a key junction between the sea and the Sahara.

Douz

In the middle of the traffic roundabout at the entrance to downtown Douz a sculpture of a camel and rider sets the tone. Douz calls itself the Gateway to the Sahara, and indeed you could wander off from the so-called *zone touristique* and lose yourself forever among the dunes. These are the genuine sand dunes of everyone's imagination, and they go off uninterruptedly to the horizon.

If tourists by the coachload come to Douz, it's no wonder. This is about as far as you can go without switching to camel or four-wheel-drive vehicle. As it is, sand encroaches on the paved roads, as if the battle with the desert is by no means under control.

Camel Country

Scores of camels-for-hire await the visitors in the *zone touristique*. They wait patiently in all postures, ready to set forth with graceful strides into the infinity of golden dunes punctuated by clumps of palms.

Thursday is market day in Douz, as remarkable for the participants—nomads, villagers and descendants of slaves—as for the exotica on sale. Not far from the market square, on the edge of the oasis, the animal market features the camel exchange.

Fights between camels are one of the highlights of the Festival of the Sahara, which takes place in Douz every December. This is also your chance to witness a fantasia, in which gun-toting, costumed horsemen simulate a wild attack, stopping just short of the audience.

Bricks are woven into geometrical patterns on the façades of Tozeur.

Chott El Jerid

Crossing the great white salt lake, the Chott El Jerid, is a haunting, unforgettable experience. The well-paved causeway starts out straightforwardly, but soon there can be mirages, whiteouts, sand-storms, perhaps hallucinations. The adventure of crossing what might as well be the Arctic Sea can't fail to touch the traveller. Incidentally, those occasional souvenir shops along the route are not mirages.

Dry most of the year, the Chott is 250 km (more than 150 miles) long and 20 km (13 miles) wide: big enough to have caught the attention of Pliny and Herodotus. Legend says the Chott is at least as treacherous as it looks: in olden days a badly navigated cara-van of 1,000 camels is said to have vanished into the mud beneath the shimmering crystal sand surface. Nowadays the fearless drivers of sailboats-on-wheels dare to cavort on the crust. They call it sand-yachting.

Tozeur

Two hundred springs refresh a couple of hundred thousand palm trees at the oasis of Tozeur, an altogether intriguing town with an international airport. The palms produce the most delicious of all dates, *deglet en-nour*, the translucent "finger of light".

Exceptional, as well, is the medieval town, in which women all in black glide along the sandy streets. The all-but-windowless walls of the houses are built of hand-made, sand-coloured bricks laid to produce geometric effects reminiscent of weaving, except that they are three-dimensional.

THE SIX BEST ROMAN RUINS You don't have to be archaeologically inclined to be moved by the sight of the Roman empire's Tunisian legacy. Suburban Carthage is easily accessible, but some of the most impressive sites are worth a journey far from modern civilization. **Dougga**: a big, stately city in a fetching site. **El Djem**: a great amphitheatre in the middle of nowhere. **Sbeitla**: sprawling ruins from late in the empire's evolution. **Bulla Regia**: theatre, temples, baths and villas. **Makhtar**: from Carthaginian to Christian influence; and an on-site museum. **Thuburbo Majus**: imperial grandeur within day-trip distance of Tunis.

Geometric and other effects also beautify the local rugs, among them designs of people and animals; these are rare in a Muslim environment where only artistic abstractions are acceptable.

Archaeological Museum

In a venerable building in the old town, the Traditional and Archaeological Museum is unsophisticated but rich in local lore. Along with regional furniture, ceramics and weapons, there is a copy of a report by a 19th-century French bureaucrat indefatigably striving to explain the distribution of water resources of the palm grove. Actually, nobody has ever bettered the elegant rationing plan of the 13th-century imam and mathematician Ibn Chabbat.

Dar Che¬rait Museum

Attached to a vast, up-market hotel, apartment and Arabian Nights theme-park development near the look-out point called the Belvedere, the Dar Cherait Museum features family heirlooms and relics of the Beys: scimitars, flintlocks and swords, and jewellery so lavish a bride would be bowed down by it. The glassware room, with a stained-glass ceiling, displays blown glass from Damascus and Bohemia.

By Tunisian standards the admission fee is expensive, but the museum is beautifully laid out, and stocked with nothing but the best.

Nefta

Halfway between Tozeur and the Algerian border, the oasis of Nefta is a place of pilgrimage of the unorthodox Sufi sect. The skyline reveals a generous helping of medieval mosques, minarets and shrines; they call it "the Kairouan of the desert". For the casual visitor, the most extraordinary sight in Nefta is the *Corbeille* (basket), a valley in the form of a bowl filled with many thousands of palms. Looking out over the top of the trees, you'd never guess all that goes on in the shadows below. Walk down the paths to discover the secrets of the hot springs, cold springs, bathing facilities and rich agricultural life.

As in Tozeur, hand-made bricks arranged in geometrical patterns distinguish the walls in the old town. In all, Nefta counts a couple of dozen mosques and scores of shrines, so the idle wanderer is bound to get an eyeful of history and architecture.

The prime religious monument, the Marabout of Sidi Bou Ali, is in the palm grove. It honours a Moroccan-born holy man who converted the local Berbers in the 13th century. Sidi Bou Ali is also credited with planting the first date palm in Nefta.

The Tunisian Desert

Tunisia's landscape has many facets. The fertile plains and cork-oak forests of the north give way to central steppes and beaches, tapering off towards the dunes of the Sahara, far beyond the Gafsa mountains and the Gulf of Gabès. The mythical south is even more diversified than the rest of the country. The desert is not a tedious, featureless expanse of sand, but in fact varies from undulating scrubland to golden dunes, from flat, seemingly infinite stretches of dusty grey soil and pebbles to pink, furrowed mountains and the sparkling white, snow-like surface of the chotts. The common denominators are the climatic influence of the Sahara and the lack of rainfall.

The desert holds many surprises in store. You can drive for hours through the wilderness, and suddenly a feathery tuft of green appears, the tousled heads of palm trees sunk in a mountain cleft. High on a hillside, a cluster of brown rocks transmutes, as you approach, into an abandoned village built of clay. A blue door in a cliffside opens to reveal the round courtyard of a troglodyte dwelling scooped out of the rock like a hobbit hole. In the depths of a hollow in the dunes, the dark rectangles of Bedouin tents cluster round a fire of palm fronds.

The village of Chenini is carved into a high cliff.

Inevitably, the winds of change are blowing over the region. You can drive for hours through the desert, then happen upon a small modern town, its die-straight dusty streets of single-storey whitewashed buildings staidly set along both sides of a grandly named Boulevard de l'Environnement. Naïve renderings of a pointy-featured Mickey Mouse decorate house walls instead of the usual good luck charms. A glimpse through the open doors reveals a carpenter's workshop, a grocery, a butcher's or a garage. The men gather in cafés or sit on the ground in a shady corner, putting the world to rights, and occasionally a woman flits past, swathed from tip to toe in an all-encompassing black haik, carrying home a bag of shopping.

In every town the biggest and finest building is the school. At all hours of the day you'll see chattering flocks of beaming children coming and going to and from classes: to solve problems of overcrowding, classes are worked in two shifts according to age.

New roads are being surfaced, while at the edge of the palm groves, sumptuous palaces of marble are surging from the sands: luxury hotels complete with swimming pools and eternally flowing fountains. Generally they are confined to a *Zone touristique* on the outskirts of town, leaving the traditional settlements intact. They are even building a golf course at Tozeur.

Berber and Arabic Heritage

The Berbers were the first to inhabit the land. Their culture has survived the centuries despite the presence or repeated invasions of other peoples from all around the Mediterranean. They settled in the southeast, at first in the plains. After the Arab conquest, however, they took refuge in the heights. All their villages are similar in appearance, citadels perching at the edge of rocky plateaux or on cliffs watching out over the coastal plain. But despite their isolation, the Berbers were unable to avoid the Arabic influence completely; during the 14th century some of them returned to the plains to form a confederation, while only the most indomitable stayed behind in their mountain redoubts. Today, for economic reasons, many have moved to the cities, where they carry on the activities specific to their village of origin.

So well do the villages blend into their background that they are hardly visible from afar. As they come into focus, they seem deserted—and indeed, many of them were abandoned long ago and left to crumble back into the earth. Others still house the descendants of tribes that have turned to a more modern, sedentary way of life, such as Douirat, once a prosperous caravan centre, Ghoumrassen, with its ghorfas and cave-dwellings, and the high citadel of Guermessa, near Tataouine.

Some of the homes, like those of Chenini, are carved into the rock face, to keep out of the relentless sun. The village layout often forms a wide amphitheatre nestling into the natural incline, layer upon layer of low houses of dry stone, linked by a dusty road. Here and there, a gateway stands proud, or the round roof of a ghorfa, the craggy ruins of a ksar or the white minaret of a mosque piercing the blue sky.

Friendly Berber from the Tataouine region, near Chenini village.

Ksour and Ghorfas

The Berber and Arab villages of the Matmata and Tataouine regions are fortified *ksour* (plural of *ksar*), which originally served as defences from enemy attack. A feature of the ksour is the *ghorfa*, a barrel-vaulted chamber where agricultural produce was stored during periods of war and raids, or whenever the villagers returned to nomadic wanderings. Generally, the most inaccessible sites were chosen: a mountain peak or a lonely outcrop in the plain. If possible, a watchtower was built to give advance warning in case of attack; this was especially useful in the region of Tataouine, which was an important post on the trans-Sahara trade route.

Though many of the ksour were abandoned or deliberately destroyed, several have been well preserved, and around Tataouine a Ksour Festival is held every year in March and April. At any time of the year you can follow an "Ksour Route" taking in some of the most impressive citadels: Ksar Haddada, a small, picturesque village whose fortress has been transformed into a hotel; Chenini, a troglodyte village where the ksar on the ridge and white mosque loom over cave dwellings gouged into the vast 55

ONE HUMP OR TWO?

Of all the desert-dwellers, from the foxy little fennec to the graceful oryx antelope, the camel remains the proud symbol of the sand dunes. In the south, herds of camels are as common as the cows of more northerly climes. Properly speaking, Tunisia's camels are dromedaries, with only one hump. Perfectly adapted to arid conditions, the animal is not a fussy eater and will content itself with nibbling a few thorny shrubs or stripped date branches. It can go without drinking for several days, filling up, when thirsty, with dozens of litres of water in a few minutes. In principle, the camel-drivers leave their beasts free to wander and find their own pastures in summer, and round them up at the water-holes. However, the dwindling numbers of nomads have automatically entailed a decline in the number of herds. The magnificent mehari, or riding camel, is now something of a tourist attraction, and wherever there are dunes, you will see these "ships of the desert" and their owners patiently waiting to take you for a ride. Don't be afraid to mount: the only time you have to hold on tight is when the creature heaves itself upright, grumbling and rumbling, pitching you forwards and backwards as it unfolds its legs in unexpected sequence. You get a great view from on high as the beast pads over the dunes, expertly guided by its owner in an arcane language of clicks and hisses. The best places for camel rides are Douz or Zaafrane, where hundreds of animals are parked at the Camel Station.

amphitheatre of the cliff face; and majestic Ksar Ouled Debbab, further south, reigning over a desolate landscape.

You will see ghorfas in every fortified enclosure and every Berber village, but the finest examples are at Metameur, where they are set on several levels around a spacious square. Of traditional design, each comprises a long, vaulted hall with just one entrance, closed by a door of palm wood. In the same area, the small town of Medenine, once an important crossroads, used to have 6,000 ghorfas. Only a few dozen remain, converted into tourist shops.

Though the ksour and ghorfas were originally built for reasons of security, they were also used, in times of peace, as community centres—markets, meetings, festivals, religious ceremonies, even school, could be held within their walls. However, the ksour never served as dwellings until modern times, when some of them have been converted into hotels.

Troglodytes

Unique to this part of North Africa, the subterranean houses of the Matmata region have become one of the main tourist attractions of the south. These unusual homes are also known as *matmata*; the name comes from a Berber tribe that once took refuge in the neighbourhood. By extension, the same term designates the principal town of the region as well as the surrounding mountain range.

The mountains appear just south of Gabès, never higher than 700 m (2,295 ft), a long row of jagged, slanting hills, separated by deep ravines supporting a sparse vegetation. The Arab-Berber population lives in humble villages clinging to the slopes, or in caves burrowed into the valleys of soft clay. Here and there, an incongruous television aerial or satellite dish sticks out of the hillside, betraying the cosy residence down below.

When setting up home, the first stage in the excavations is to dig a hole up to 10 m (33 ft) deep, which will serve as the main courtyard. Then any number of rooms are carved out from the surrounding rock wall—which provides plenty of scope for later additions as the family increases. The kitchen, bedrooms, living rooms and larders are set on the lower level, and above them, reached by a rope ladder, smaller caves serve as storehouses, linked to the exterior by sloping, narrow channels through which the grain is poured. Tunnels and labyrinthine staircases lead off the main courtyard to other rooms used as stables or toolsheds. The temperature is constant: cool during 57 the day and warm at night, but the windowless rooms are dark and stuffy.

Matmata is the best-known troglodyte village, and has several well-equipped underground hotels. But you will discover similar villages in the region, such as Techine, inhabited by sedentarized Bedouins.

Desert and Chott

Conforming more to the conventional image of the desert, the Tunisian South does, in certain places, consist of vast empty spaces where camel trains plod the sands from one oasis to another. But from the Algerian frontier to the Far South, even on the Mediterranean shores, the oases and deserts have individual characters.

A great expanse of steppe lies between the fertile north and the south, where all the agriculture depends on the oases. Low in the eastern coastal zone and high in the west, this has always been nomad land; the pastures are meagre and the soil difficult to work. The main crop is esparto grass, used since time immemorial for weaving and basket-making.

You will notice the transition once past Gafsa, as you enter the Jerid. In a region that once grew prosperous from the slave trade, the steppe gradually gives way to

a stony desert. Grey, scrawny bushes speckle the cracked earth that later disintegrates into boundless stretches of sand. The rolling dunes of the Great Eastern Erg, 50–80 m (165–260 ft) high, change colour as the sun beats down, playing games with the shadows, while the hot, dry sirocco (or chélili), laden with sand and dust, constantly remodels their shapes. An attempt to anchor them down with fences of palm branches has met with some success.

Before you reach the desert of sand, you have to cross the desert of salt. El Jerid is the largest of the chotts, immense depressions that sweep across the entire width of the country, shifting masses of slimy mud and sand. As soon as the temperature increases to more than 30°C (86°F), a misty vapour rises, renowned for inducing mirages. Brilliant white salt crystals form a thick crust on the surface, sometimes crisp and dry like fresh snow, sometimes wet and slushy. At the edges of the chott, and at certain periods of the year, the salt is submerged by a shallow layer of water.

A road across Chott El Jerid links the two important oases of

Villagers of Matmata keep cool and cosy in their grotto-like homes.

The Sahara—a vast expanse of dunes undulating beyond the horizon.

Tozeur and Douz. It runs parallel to the old camel route, marked by poles that still stick up here and there. The road is dotted with incongruous souvenir stands selling sand roses dyed in lurid green, pink and blue.

Beneath the Palms

Cool, shaded gardens where fruit and vegetables grow, the whisper of palm fronds rustling in the wind, the song of trickling water, a green-gold light stealing through the leaves: such is the magical charm of the oasis.

Flourishing beneath the desert skies, the oases were formed spontaneously, wherever condi-

tions permitted. They range from tiny patches of green clustered around water holes at the base of arid cliffs, through regiments of trees forming a fringe along a river valley, to vast palm groves spreading over huge areas.

Whatever their environment, the one thing they all have in common is the presence of water. Gushing out of springs, coursing down the *oueds* (wadies) or accumulated beneath the surface as ground water, it is essential to life in the desert. And paradoxically, there's plenty of it, if you know where to look. The precious element is divided into several types. Spring or well water is reserved

60

for human consumption, while the cattle drink the still water of the pools, also used for washing and laundry. Irrigation water is collected in clay-lined holding tanks, from which it pours into main channels, *seguias*, branching off into secondary *masraf*, the furrows that delineate each vegetable patch. The cycle is completed by an ingenious underground drainage system, the *khettara*.

Another feature of all oases—and also essential to life in the desert—is the date palm. This graceful tree grows to a height of 30 m (100 ft), its roots tapping the water from the underground lakes, and its head in the sun. Beneath its branches grow great clusters of nourishing fruit, the most prized variety being *deglet en-nour*, "fingers of light". Harvested in autumn and exported world-wide, these choice thin-skinned golden dates form the staple food of the local population. The "seconds" are fed to the livestock: the donkeys, pigs, goats, even the chickens and turkeys are fattened on this sweet fruit. Every part of the plant serves a useful purpose: the trunks for building and furniture-making, the leaves for thatching and fencing, basketmaking and wrapping food for cooking. The fruiting branches or bouquets, once stripped of dates, can be made into brooms or given to the camels to munch. The stones are used for fuel, while the sharp leaf ribs make ideal skewers for cooking chunks of meat over a fire of fronds. The thorns come in handy as toothpicks.

The palm canopy forms a filter protecting the orchards below: figs, olives, almonds, peaches, apricots, pomegranates, mandarin oranges, and so on, thrive in the shade. At ground level, the land is divided into allotments separated by a maze of low walls (*tabia*) providing year-round supplies of carrots, turnips, tomatoes, onions, courgettes and watermelons, grown in rotation. A patchwork of larger plots are sown with wheat, corn and other grain.

All the houses are built outside the palm grove in a more arid one, as every scrap of fertile land is carefully reserved for cultivation.

Oasis Routes

Coming from the north, in the direction of Tozeur, the first real oasis you reach after the high plains is Gafsa. It may be called the Rose of the Desert, but don't expect too much—it's the centre of a phosphate mining industry. There is, however, a palm grove at the entrance to the town.

Metlaoui, a former nomad encampment, is now a phosphate-mining town with a population of

27,000. If you arrive at Metlaoui in the morning, you can catch the 10.30 *Lézard Rouge*, the grand old train of the Bey, which does a 2-hour return trip through the spectacular orange gash of the Seldja Gorge. You could almost believe you have travelled back in time and space to the Wild West, as your mahogany and leather-upholstered carriage rattles through the narrow defile and into the arid and dramatic rock-strewn landscape.

Mountain Oases

West of Metlaoui are the mountain oases, easily reached by a surfaced road. You can seen the green strip of Chebika's palm grove from afar, contrasting with the ochre backdrop of the mountains. Springs tumble down from on high, feeding a wadi and several gorges, and there's an old abandoned village which you might like to visit for the view it affords over the desert.

A few kilometres further along a winding road, Tamerza, with its refreshing waterfall, would make the perfect setting for a Western. The old village of rich red-brown mud bricks, abandoned after flooding, is fast returning into dust. You can get a good view of it from the modern hotel built on the hillside opposite.

Last stop before the Algerian frontier, the forsaken village of Midès, trapped between two mountain slopes, seems to be suspended over a void. The nearby palm and orange groves provide welcome shade.

Desert Oases

Southwest of Metlaoui, the oases of the Jerid are completely different in character. Tozeur and Nefta were once important stopovers for the trans-Sahara caravans. But here, the land is flat and abundantly watered by dozens of springs. Nefta's palm grove has some 400,000 trees, while that of Tozeur counts well over a million. The water drains off into the nearby chotts, in particular the famous Chott El Jerid, gateway to the desert oases.

As the chott gives way to firmer ground, you pass several small oases strung out along the sand-swept road, and soon the first dunes appear. Kebili, the administrative capital of the region, is an old Berber town. It was long known for its important slave market, where captives brought by caravan from Sudan were sold.

Further south is Douz, the most typically "Saharan" of the Tunisian oases. This unpretentious

Memories of medieval Tunisia at a desert festival. Old wars were simpler but fervently fought.

desert town, surrounded by dunes whipped into an infinite variety of shapes by the wind, remains fondly attached to the ancestral traditions of the M'razig tribes: breeding desert hounds; selling Berber jewellery and handicrafts made from camel hide in its Thursday market; staging the annual festival of the Sahara over Christmas and the New Year, staged in a purpose-built stadium. Douz is the guardian of the Great Erg, and a meeting place for nomads and oasis dwellers.

Nearby, other oases such as Nouil and Zaafrane struggle to survive against the wind and encroaching sand. From Zaafrane you can hire a dromedary for a trip into the desert for several days, or just an hour or two. Farther away, to the southeast, Ksar Ghilane is the last stop before the Sahara.

From Douz, you can drive to the coast by the northern route meandering round the Djebel Tebaga, or take the new road via Matmata to Gabès. Whichever one you choose, you pass through a surprising landscape of sand, pebbles and thorny scrub grazed by herds of camels. They tend to amble aimlessly across the road, so drive carefully.

SURVIVING THE DESERT

Whether you're travelling by car, coach or camel, remember to protect yourself from the heat. You will need sunglasses, lightweight, light-coloured clothing, and comfortable walking shoes or hiking boots, and a hat or long scarf to wind into a turban (the Tunisians leave one end hanging down to protect the back of the neck). The temperature drops dramatically after dark, so you will need something warm. Make sure you have plenty of water to drink.

If you have decided to discover the Tunisian South on your own, you should take a few elementary precautions. Make sure your vehicle is in good condition, and considering the distance between petrol stations, fill the tank as soon as it is half empty. Take plenty of water, and do no venture onto difficult desert tracks without any equipment; ask around for advice beforehand. If your car breaks down, do not go wandering off to find help. Stay beside your vehicle as it will be the only shelter you have from the sun. Avoid driving at night (there are no lights, no white lines and no road signs to guide you); go slowly, watch out for potholes, other vehicles, people and animals straying over the road.

You're bound to find just the right carpet in Tozeur's souk.

Maritime Oases

The maritime oases range along the Mediterranean coast, a harmonious picture of blue sea, green palm trees and golden beaches. In the 100 km (60 miles) between Oudhref (reputed for its carpets) and Zarzis, and on the luxuriant island of Djerba, there are several palm groves worth visiting.

The biggest and most accessible is that of Gabès, a mainly industrial city with some 300,000 date palms stretching for 6 km (4 miles) down to the coast. The most attractive area is at Chenini, to the west; you can hire a horse-drawn carriage near the bus station (or walk). Chenini is the epitome of an oasis village, perfectly organized in three layers of date palms, fruit trees and tobacco and herbs at their foot, with a special drainage system to evacuate the water and siphon off the salt which would otherwise burn the soil.

From Gabès, travel along the coastal plain to visit the other maritime oases such as Mareth and its neighbour Zarat, before ending your journey at Zarzis, a not particularly pretty town surrounded by olive groves, but with several large package hotels to the north, set in gardens giving directly onto the beach.

65

Cultural Notes

In spite of all its comforts and conveniences, Tunisia is a very foreign country. For many first-time visitors the initial few days are the cultural equivalent of stepping off a centrifuge, or walking out of a dark room into the tropical sun: dizzying and blinding and thoroughly disorientating. A few brief pointers for understanding:

Islam. Although Tunisian history goes back to the Phoenicians, the most momentous influence is much more recent. Islam, the youngest of the world's major religions, is never far from the surface. (But long before the prophet Mohammed heard the words of God in the 7th century, desert people believed in a single supreme being.) "Islam" literally means "submission" (to God, or Allah).

Pillars. The Koran details the Five Pillars of Islam, backbone of the faith: Reciting the creed, "There is no god but God, and Mohammed is his prophet." Praying five times daily and in the mosque on Friday. Giving to charity. Respecting the rules of abstinence and piety of the holy month of Ramadan. And finally, making a pilgrimage to Mecca at least once in a lifetime.

Mosques. Non-Muslims are barred from the prayer-halls of mosques. But the courtyards are often open to inspection, and from them you may be able to get a glimpse of the atmosphere within. Although the columns and chandeliers can be lavish, the only ornaments are arabesque designs and elaborate calligraphy. The Koran proscribes representations of living things, so Islamic art developed in other, more abstract directions. However, museums sometimes reveal centuries'-old portraits or animal scenes that were commissioned by rulers or aristocrats for their personal collections.

Muezzin. The faithful are called to their prayers five times a day, starting before dawn, by the voice of the muezzin emanating from the heights of the minaret, usually by loudspeaker, perhaps pre-recorded. Mohammed himself is said to have created the job, reasoning that the human voice would be preferable to any variation on the bells and horns sounded by Christians or Jews.

Hammams. When attached to mosques, hammams are ritual baths. Elsewhere in town, they're a place for gregarious cleanliness—usually a men's club in the morning and for women in the afternoon. The Romans were first to make a pleasure and a ritual out of a bath. The Turkish bath style in Tunisia is often finished off by a massage and a nap.

Charity. Alms-giving once was a prescribed percentage of one's wealth, but now it's a matter of general generosity to the less fortunate, as encouraged in the Koran. Beggars—you'll see them squatting outside a mosque or in the market—don't have to be pushy because they know Allah will send enough benefactors their way.

Women. Many Muslim men cite the Koran to justify segregating their women, and for making sure they are very fully clothed from chin to ankles when they appear in public. Modern Tunisia outlaws polygamy, gives women the vote and other rights, and puts them far ahead of their sisters in other Arab countries, but tradition-bound villagers drag their feet on the road to full emancipation.

Weddings. Even though the mosque is not involved, a traditional marriage in Tunisia is a stately celebration that goes on for days. For the occasion the women of the family drop everything to prepare and beautify the bride (hennaed hands and soles of feet are considered the last word in desirability). Hand-woven wedding gowns, so heavy the bride can barely move, can be unbelievably ornate. The processions are motorized and very noisy.

Music. Don't try to make sense of Arabic music at the outset; just let it wash over you until something eventually clicks—perhaps you'll hear an echo of the wail of an Andalusian flamenco. The voice is accompanied by a lute, plus perhaps a fiddle and a dulcimer. Minor keys don't have to be sad.

Holidays. The big Tunisian holidays have no link with the seasons, for they are religious observances based on the lunar calendar. The holy month of Ramadan requires fasting from sun-up to sunset, a tougher regime in summer than in winter. Nightfall brings rousing celebrations that more than compensate for the asceticism, and the solemn month concludes with the family feast of Aid el Seghir. The commemoration of Abraham's sacrifice, Aid el Adha, is another festive time for children, though the mass slaughter of sheep isn't everybody's cup of tea. The Prophet's birthday, Mouled, is marked with feasting and firecrackers, especially in Kairouan. 67

Shopping

Even unenthusiastic shoppers tend to succumb to the souvenirs of Tunisia, as useful as sponges, spices and salad bowls, or as improbable as a water pipe. The workmanship may not be the finest in the world, but what's important is the memory—of the place you found your gift, the face of the artisan, or at least the glint in the eye of the salesman.

Souks and Shops

Here is an understatement: prices in the souks are not fixed. The sky's the limit on the price asked, whereas the *real* selling price, attained after laborious negotiations, may be but a small fraction of the starting quotation. Even if your heart's not in it, you have to haggle in the souks, for it's part of the ritual and the fun. But don't waste the merchant's time if you're not really interested; tell him so with a smile and walk away before you've been plied with coffee and super-salesmanship.

People who can't handle haggling should patronize state-run, fixed-price gift shops operated by ONAT, the *Office National de l'Artisanat de Tunisie*. Spacious

and welcoming, these are well stocked with a cross-section of Tunisian handicrafts, and the knowledgeable assistants speak several languages. If you're in a rush, there's no better way to pick up the right gift. But if you want to experience "real life" and take home a story along with a souvenir, check the price tag at ONAT, then try your luck in the fragrant alleys of the old town.

Good Ideas

Tunisian carpets come in many versions, from the most luxurious and intricate to the rough and folksy, big enough for anybody's living room or small enough for a doorstep. *Carpets* are composed of knotted strands, with the most prized ones having the most knots per square metre. Less complex, hence less expensive, are woven *kilims*. Another category is the *mergoum*, a kilim with overstitched geometric

No two pots exactly alike: artisan in Guellala, Djerba, keeps alive the village's ancient tradition.

designs. Kairouan and Gafsa are famous for the quality of their carpets. Other good sources are Tozeur, Gabès and Djerba.

Animal...

Leather goods are everywhere you look, but the quality varies wildly. You'll be offered everything from a saddle to a handbag to Arabian-nights-style slippers.

Sheepskins are sold in souvenir shops as well as in less polished form at country butchers' shops along the side of the road.

Sea sponges appear for sale authentically in places such as Djerba, where they are cleaned, dried and trimmed before being presented to the public.

Vegetable...

Baskets of all shapes and sizes and uses are made from esparto grass or palm fronds. The same craftsmen also produce sun hats and table mats. Olive wood is carved into anything from a fully equipped chess board to a pocketable camel figurine. Food products are a useful souvenir—olive oil, harissa sauce, dates, and herbs like saffron and coriander in basic plastic bags.

Mineral

The Tunisian souvenir industry exploits an expressive form of crystallized gypsum in the sand rose or *rose du Sahara*, dug out of the sandy soil in the south. What you do with this decorative rock when you get home is a test of ingenuity. More expensive minerals like gold and silver go into the jewellery, which is confected in Tunis, Sousse, Sfax and Djerba. Popular good-luck charms come in the form of a fish or the Hand of Fatima. Copper and brass plates, bowls or ashtrays are decorated before your eyes by artisans chipping away in full view in the souk.

Ceramics craftsmen are centred in Nabeul and Djerba, the latter specializing in less elaborate pots and amusing novelties. Among other specialities, Nabeul offers Andalusian-style painted tiles.

More Ideas

The Tunisian version of a fez, the red felt *chechia,* is considerably more portable. Or pick up a hooded *burnoose* to remind you of desert sands long after you're home. Collectible dolls in local costumes come in a great variety; the Gabès doll in red is as different from the Sousse girl all wrapped up in white as a kilt is from jeans. Berber dolls are carved of wood—fierce-faced characters, some with scimitars. Graceful white and blue birdcages from Sidi Bou Saïd are very popular; you don't even have to own a bird.

Dining Out

Tunisian cuisine is hearty and wholesome and usually excellent value for money. If your appetite needs encouraging, a tour of the nearest market should be an inspiration, for the vegetables and fish here are fresher and more alluring than almost anywhere. And just sniff those spices! Typical Tunisian food is derived from Arabic, Turkish and, to a lesser extent, French sources. International specialities are widely available, too.

On the Menu

The most typically Tunisian dish, *couscous,* is delicious and full of flavour and character. The base is a whopping portion of delicately rolled grains of semolina. On top are stewed lamb, chicken or fish, and chickpeas, red peppers, potatoes, cabbage and eggs. In the unlikely event that it's not spicy enough, add some *harissa* to taste.

A vegetable stew, *chakchouka,* features ingredients as simple as onions, tomatoes, chick peas and peppers, often surmounted by a fried egg. In general, vegetarians may be hard pressed to find acceptable dishes in the typical Tunisian restaurant.

An egg, sometimes quite runny, is the surprising ingredient in a *brik,* a popular starter or street-corner snack. It is popped into a thin pastry envelope, surrounded by spicy vegetables, tuna, or just a few capers, then deep-fried until crisp and golden.

Mechoui (pronounced *mish-wee*) describes an array of grilled meats, mostly lamb, the details varying from restaurant to restaurant. Mechoui is one of the dishes that may include *merguez,* small red mutton sausages seasoned with mint—quite hot and spicy.

Mechouia, not to be confused with mechoui, is an appetizer with originality, including hard-boiled eggs, tuna, olives and capers, cooked and then cooled and served as a salad.

Another potential confusion: Tunisian *tajine* bears little resemblance to the rich meat-and-vegetable stew of the same name famed elsewhere in North Africa; here it is rather like a quiche or soufflé or omelette.

Fish and Seafood

Many visiting gourmets find the fresh fish a real highlight of the Tunisian coast. A variety of desirable Mediterranean species, just out of the net, may be displayed in a refrigerated case or on a platter in the dining room. Generally menus use the French names—*mérou* (grouper), *rouget* (red mullet), *loup de mer* (perch), *daurade* (sea bream) and so on. But you can just point at the one that looks best and it will be grilled in your honour.

Shellfish, too, is abundant—*moules* (mussels), *huîtres* (oysters), *crevettes* (prawns), and, expensively but great for a treat, *langouste* (rock lobster).

Sweets

The sweets in Tunisia are overwhelmingly sweet. Thank the Turks for *baklawa,* a flaky honey-and-nuts splurge. *Loukoum* is the Tunisian version of Turkish delight. *Kab el ghazal* is an almond-filled horn of pastry—*corne de gazelle* in French.

Fresh fruit is a refreshing antidote to honey-rich desserts. Depending on the season, you'll delight in the local melons, strawberries, dates and cherries.

Wines

The Carthaginians and Romans had a way with grapes, and so do modern Tunisians (with a helping hand from the French). They produce eminently potable wines of all persuasions, and usually at attractive prices. A few labels to look for:

Blanc de blancs, a breathtakingly dry white wine that's perfect with fish.

Muscat sec de Kelibia, an original white reminiscent of retsina.

Château Feriani, a full-bodied red from the "côte d'Utica".

Haut Mornag, a dry, light red.

El Kahena, a refreshing rosé.

Gris de Tunisie, another good bet for rosé fans.

Beer lovers have few complaints about *Celtia,* the light Tunisian lager. Alternatively, expensive imports are sometimes available.

Several brands of mineral waters, flat or fizzy, are served in cafés and restaurants.

Brandy fanciers will want to sip a sample of the local specialities: *boukka,* a fig brandy, and *thibarine,* an aromatic date liqueur.

At the Café

Tunisians are hooked on coffee. Cafés serve it in many forms, from espresso to café au lait to thick, sweet Turkish-style coffee. A popular alternative for passing the time is *thé à la menthe*—mint tea, produced differently at each café; the colour can be yellow or brown, a sprig of fresh mint may or may not float on the surface. 73

Sports

To work off some of the calories acquired from couscous and honey-oozing sweets, you can choose from a generous menu of sports. Or jog along the beach or do a few laps in the pool.

On Sea

Fishing has rich possibilities here. Anyone can go after the big ones, from the beach or a pier or bobbing about in a dinghy. No permit is necessary. Charters can be organized from almost any harbour.

About 30 ports from Tabarka in the northwest to Zarzis in the far south are geared for pleasure boats. There are showcase marina complexes at Port El Kantaoui, Cap Monastir, Sidi Bou Saïd and Tabarka. Resort hotels cater to the needs of most water sports enthusiasts, notably windsurfers, water-skiers and sailors.

Scuba divers converge on Tabarka's coral reef. Other dive centers are at Port El Kantaoui and Monastir with tuition and equipment available.

On Land

Like the population, golf in Tunisia is concentrated near the coast, from Tabarka in the north to the newest course on the isle of Djerba, designed by British architect Martin Hawtree. The layout at Tabarka exploits a sensational position amidst pine and eucalyptus trees alongside the sea. The architect, California's Ronald Fream, also designed the courses in the resorts of Hammamet, Monastir and Port El Kantaoui. There's more golf at Sousse, and in the Tunis area at Soukra and Gammarth, and a desert course is under construction in Tozeur.

Hundreds of tennis courts adjoin resort hotels and sports clubs all over the country.

Horse-riding may take you through olive groves or alongside the Mediterranean. For a more exotic mount, hop aboard a camel for a jaunt along the beach or, if you're really serious, several days among the dunes on an escorted trek from oasis to oasis.

In autumn and winter, hunting expeditions are mounted in the Tunisian hills, with wild boar the principal target. It's essential to organize the logistics well in advance.

The Hard Facts

On the countdown to your trip, here are a few essential points you ought to know about Tunisia:

Airports

Tunisia's principal aerial gateways are Tunis, Monastir and Djerba. There are also international airports at Sfax, Tozeur and Tabarka. All the usual facilities are provided, from baggage trolleys and porters (no payment necessary) to banks and car-hire desks. There are duty-free shops for both incoming and outgoing passengers.

Climate

Much of the country enjoys a mild Mediterranean climate. The coastal zones, where the tourists and most of the population hang out, bask in largely sunny winters and dry, hot summers. In the capital, Tunis, the lowest temperature ever recorded was −1°C (30°F). But the average January temperature is a gentle 10°C (50°F). In July it's 26°C (79°F). Hardly any rain falls between May and September. It gets hotter and drier the farther south you go. And inland, heading toward the Sahara, summer temperatures go well past 40°C (above 100°F). The lack of humidity is a boon.

Communications

Local, national and international telephone service is good. You can dial directly from most phones to overseas numbers. It's usually cheaper to go to the telephone office of the post office (PTT) or use a pay phone (Taxiphone) rather than calling from your hotel room. To make an international call, dial 00 then the country code (1 for US and Canada, 44 for UK, 353 for Ireland), then the area code without the initial zero, and the local number. Hotels and post offices often have telefax facilities, as well, and there are Internet cafés for your e-mails. The postal service works efficiently; out-bound postcards usually reach destinations in Europe within a week. You can buy stamps wherever postcards are sold, though for philatelic variety the post office is a better bet.

Complaints

Most problems can be worked out on the spot with a smile and a shrug, but for difficult cases take your complaint to someone 75 in charge—the maître d'hôtel in a restaurant or the manager of a hotel. If you think you've been overcharged by a vendor in the souk it's probably too late to change anything.

Crime

You may feel hemmed in in the seething, narrow alleys of the medina, but you're probably safer than on most city streets in Europe. To avoid tempting fate, though, leave your valuables in the hotel safe. Don't invite any potential pickpockets by carrying an open handbag or wearing a wallet on your hip.

Currency

The unit of currency is the Tunisian dinar (abbreviated D or TUD). In an odd departure from the decimal system, the dinar is divided into a thousand millimes. Thus a price of five dinars would be written 5.000 D. Tourists are unlikely to come across any coins smaller than 50 or 100 millimes; coins go on up to a half-dinar and 1 dinar. Banknotes are mostly found in denominations of 5 and 10 dinars. Banks have 20- and 30- dinar notes but they're rare on the street.

Well-known brands of credit cards are accepted in places where tourists congregate, including leading restaurants and hotels. Banks and hotels cash travellers cheques. Be sure to hold on to the exchange receipt, which you'll need if you want to change unspent dinars into foreign currency on departure. (In any case, the maximum you can reconvert is 100 dinars.)

Driving

As in continental Europe, drive on the right. The roads are good, and getting better. Tunisians are generally careful drivers, respectful of others and the speed limits—50 km per hour in towns, 70 on the isle of Djerba and 90 elsewhere in the country (110 on the motorway). One reason for their caution is the frequency of police checks. In addition to the patrol cars on the highways, road blocks are set up on the edge of many towns and villages. Courteous police officers may want to inspect the car's papers, or just wave you past. (Or one of them may be hitching a ride.)

Driving through almost any town or village requires great concentration and tact, because pedestrians and livestock wander all over the streets; cyclists also claim as their own a broad section of the roadway. Direction signs on the highway are good, mostly bilingual French-Arabic, though it may take time to get used to the long distance between a sign and the intersection it announces. City parking is straightforward, with meters in the busiest places but otherwise a relaxed atmosphere.

Emergencies

The universal telephone number for the police is 197. But the best place to start is your hotel desk, which can handle many problems. In complex cases, consult your consulate.

Essentials

Virtually anything you might need is available in Tunisia, but if you always take prescribed drugs be sure to carry your own. The Tunisian version might have a different name or dosage. For your packing checklist: sunscreen lotion, insect repellent and a sun hat. As for clothing, don't forget a sweater for winter nights. On the beaches, fashions are as anywhere else along the Mediterranean, but modest dress is appropriate in town. Women might want to pack long skirts and long-sleeved tops.

Formalities

Most tourists need only a valid passport or national identity card to visit Tunisia.

On arrival you'll probably be waved through the Customs inspection. For the record, all passengers, irrespective of age, are allowed to bring in 200 cigarettes or 50 cigars or 400 g tobacco,

1 bottle of wine or spirits, a reasonable quantity of perfume and gifts up to a value of 10 dinars. You can import an unlimited amount of foreign currency and export up to the equivalent of 500 dinars, but the local currency itself can be neither imported nor exported.

Health

No inoculations are compulsory for Tunisia, but it's wise to ask your family doctor whether he recommends a round of shots, especially if you're going to wander in the south. You'll want to sign up for a travel health insurance policy before you leave home. Too much sun is a danger on any beach holiday, especially in southern latitudes, for palefaces who overdo the tanning efforts from the first day. To avoid unpleasant consequences, start with early morning and late afternoon sunbathing and wear a sun hat and sunscreen lotion. Water is generally drinkable but it's prudent to order bottled mineral water. Restaurants try to maintain high hygienic standards. In the event of an upset any pharmacy will prescribe remedial pills. At least one chemist's in every city stays open all night.

Holidays and Festivals

Two calendars are used—the standard Gregorian model of 365

days as well as the Muslim year, which is 11 days shorter.

Non-religious public holidays:

January 1	New Year
March 20	Independence Day
March 21	Youth Day
April 9	Martyrs' Day
May 1	Labour Day
July 25	Republic Day
August 13	Women's Day
November 7	National Day

Moveable holidays:

Hegire	New Year
El Mouled	Birthday of the Prophet Muhammad
Eid el-Fitr	End of Ramadan
Eid el-Idha	Feast of the Sacrifice

In addition, various regions hold festivals and colourful manifestations at different times of year.

Languages

Arabic is the official language but fluent French is widely spoken, even in remote villages. Your school French will come in handy, if only for reading menus and the signs on shops. English speakers are found in many areas.

Newspapers

Tunisia's French-language newspapers such as *La Presse de Tunisie* offer a sampling of the international news, listings of local events and exchange rates. The weekly *Tunisia News* is printed in English. Foreign newspapers (in English, French, German, Italian, Spanish and Dutch) are sold in Tunis and major resorts, at best a day after publication.

Opening hours

Bankers' hours are eccentric in Tunisia; luckily, you can change money almost any time at your hotel. In summer (actually July to the end of August), banks open only in the mornings, Monday to Friday from 7.30 to 11.30 a.m. (In tourist areas one bank opens Saturday mornings as well.) In winter, the five mornings a week schedule continues, but banks re-open for a couple of hours in the afternoon. During Ramadan the schedule is 8 to 11.30 a.m. and 1 to 2.30 p.m.

Post offices generally open Monday to Friday 7.30 or 8 a.m.–noon. In winter they re-open in late afternoon and on Saturday mornings.

Shops are unpredictable; many close for siesta in summer—say, from noon to 3 p.m.—then stay open into the early evening.

Most museums close Monday.

Social graces

Hospitality comes naturally to the smiling Tunisians, who are always ready to help a visitor in distress or momentarily lost. Hand-shaking is as commonplace as saying hello. If you can learn a phrase or two in Arabic, it will spark the most enthusiastic reactions.

Both dress and behaviour are modest in this country where most women are covered from chin to ankle. Anywhere away from the hotel, visitors—both men and women—would do well to cover knees and chests.

Television
Many hotels have satellite dishes piping in international TV networks such as CNN, Sky News and BBC World. Local programmes are in both Arabic and French.

Time
Tunisia now observes daylight saving time, so it is always one hour ahead of Britain, GMT +1 in winter and GMT+2 in summer.

Tipping
Taxi drivers, waiters and hotel personnel are always ready to receive a tip for services rendered—say, 10 per cent in a restaurant, more at the hairdresser's. When in doubt, tip as you would anywhere else; the worst you can do is brighten up someone's day.

Toilets
There are no municipally operated public conveniences. The best thing to do in times of need is head for a reasonably luxurious hotel or restaurant. If there's an attendant, a small tip is expected. The facilities in local cafés are unlikely to come up to your standards. Veteran travellers always carry some toilet tissue.

Transport
Getting around Tunisia can involve just about every means of transport from air-conditioned coaches to indefatigable camels. You can cut long distances aboard a domestic airline flight (there are airports at Tunis, Monastir, Djerba, Sfax, Tozeur, Tabarka, El Borma, Gabes and Gafsa), take a comfortable train, or rent a car or four-wheel-drive jeep. Colourful communal taxis, called *louages,* provide fast intercity links—sometimes heart-stoppingly fast. For city travel there are plenty of taxis, buses and, in Tunis, a modern métro—actually a light railway system, running above ground. A métro also connects the cities of Sousse and Monastir.

Voltage
With a few exceptions, 220-volt, 50-cycle AC is the standard nationwide. Sockets take two round pins.

INDEX

GENERAL EDITOR
  Barbara Ender-Jones
LAYOUT
  André Misteli
TEXT TUNISIAN DESERT
  Michel Puysségur
PHOTO CREDITS
  Guiziou/hemis.fr: front cover, pp. 2, 5, 6, 11, 12, 21, 26, 28, 36, 42, 49, 60, 65
  Barbier/hemis.fr: p. 24
  Frances/hemis.fr: pp. 30, 59
  Wysocki/hemis.fr: pp. 52, 55
  Rieger/hemis.fr: p. 56
  Bernard Joliat: p. 16
  Claude Huber: back cover, pp. 9, 32, 63, 68
  CORBIS/Wheeler: p. 38
  CORBIS/Garrett: p. 72
MAPS
  Elsner & Schichor
  JPM Publications

Copyright © 2006, 1994
by JPM Publications S.A.
12, avenue William-Fraisse,
1006 Lausanne, Switzerland
information@jpmguides.com
www.jpmguides.com/

Printed in Switzerland
Weber/Bienne (CTP) – 10199.00.0231
Edition 2006–2007